THE RIVERS CHELMER
AND
BLACKWATER

THE RIVERS CHELMER
AND
BLACKWATER

BY

STAN JARVIS

TERENCE DALTON LIMITED
LAVENHAM   .   SUFFOLK
1990

Published by
TERENCE DALTON LIMITED

ISBN 0 86138 083 5

Text photoset in 10/12pt Baskerville

Printed in Great Britain at
The Lavenham Press Limited, Lavenham, Suffolk

Contents

Foreword

By Admiral Sir Andrew Lewis
HM Lord Lieutenant of Essex

ALMOST ten years ago I wrote the foreword to Stan Jarvis's book *A View into Essex*, which in the intervening years has given me and countless other people from the county and far beyond much pleasure, so I was delighted to receive the author's invitation to write a foreword to his latest book, in which he traces the course of two Essex rivers, the Chelmer and the Blackwater. The latter, known to me and my neighbours as the Pant, passes close to my own home. Thus he takes us through some of the loveliest parts of the county and tells us of many Essex men and women who lived in the area, people as diverse as Dick Turpin and Daisy, Countess of Warwick. It is a fascinating book from the pen of one who has become a true chronicler of the county, and I recommend it with great confidence.

Andrew Lewis, Finchingfield.

Acknowledgements

SCORES of people have paused in the pursuit of their own interests to answer our questions. Some have gone to the trouble of corresponding with us, sending information and photographs. I thank particularly Anglian Water, Geoff Baker, Chief Photographer of the Essex Chronicle, Jenny Ball of Marconi Sailing Club, Bradwell Power Station, Mr and Mrs S. Brice, Mrs C. Brown, Peter Came, Vernon Clarke, Mrs C. Down, Essex County Council Highways Department, Essex Water Company, Vic Gray, the County Archivist, and his staff, Mr and Mrs I. Haig of Tiptofts, Mr and Mrs Kirk of Mundon Hall, Langford Golf Club, the Reverend K. Howell of Tollesbury, Mr Padfield of Wimbish Hall Farm, Ron Patient, my friend in photography, Ted Pearson of Anglian Water, T. D. Ridley & Sons Ltd, Alan Shadrack, the Reverend W. J. Smith of Boreham, Mrs F. Spurrier, Mr and Mrs P. Tuck of Barnes Mill, Bill Ward of *Forward* and David Waugh of Chelmsford Library.

There are many more people who, unnamed though they may be, are thanked most sincerely. Last, but not least, we gratefully acknowledge the help and the encouragement of Elisabeth Whitehair and her team of experts at Terence Dalton.

Introduction

Choice Chelmer comes along, a Nymph most neatly clear,
Which well-near through the midst doth cut the wealthy sheere.
By Dunmow gliding down to Chelmsford holds her chase,
To which she gives the name, which as she doth embrace
Clear Can comes tripping in, and doth with Chelmer close:
With whose supply (though small as yet) she greater grows.
She for old Maldon makes, where in her passing by,
She to remembrance calls that Roman colony.
When Chelmer scarce arrives in her most wish'd bay,
But Blackwater comes in, through many a crooked way,
Which Pant was called of yore; but that, by Time exiled,
She Freshwell after hight, then Blackwater instyled.

                    Michael Drayton: *Polyolbion*, 1622

THE CHELMER is thirty-five miles long. It rises in Rowney Wood in the parish of Debden. The Blackwater, or Pant, is thirty-three miles long and rises at Frogs Green on the edge of the adjoining parish of Wimbish. They have been canalized over the lower part of their courses to form the Chelmer and Blackwater navigation. These are the basic facts in verse and prose; the bones of a story which, when fleshed out, presents many differing aspects of these two rivers.

The fact that from the earliest times they afforded ancient man his very "water of life" gave the rivers a significance which passed from worship of them as spirits in pagan religion to an important place in the realms of folklore and so on down to our time with the old adage that there was nothing an Englishman liked better than messing about in boats. A lingering reverence of rivers is understandable upon consideration of just how long man has lived in close association with them. He drank their waters gratefully, he mixed their mud to make primitive pottery to store that water. He travelled inland easily on their main streams and their tributaries to fan out over the land. As man's skills developed he irrigated his crops, drove his mills, tanned his leather, laid his osier beds and developed a hundred and one other crafts with their help. Many places owe their names to the rivers which watered them or where they were safe to cross, such as Shalford and Heybridge.

Man's dependence on these two rivers down to this day is reflected in the fact that thirty-six per cent of the water suipplied by the Essex Water Company is drawn from the Chelmer and the Blackwater.

The rivers ran free for hundreds of years, tolerated because man had no answer to their awesome power. Gradually though, like the breaking in of mettlesome horses, the rivers were tamed in the service of man.

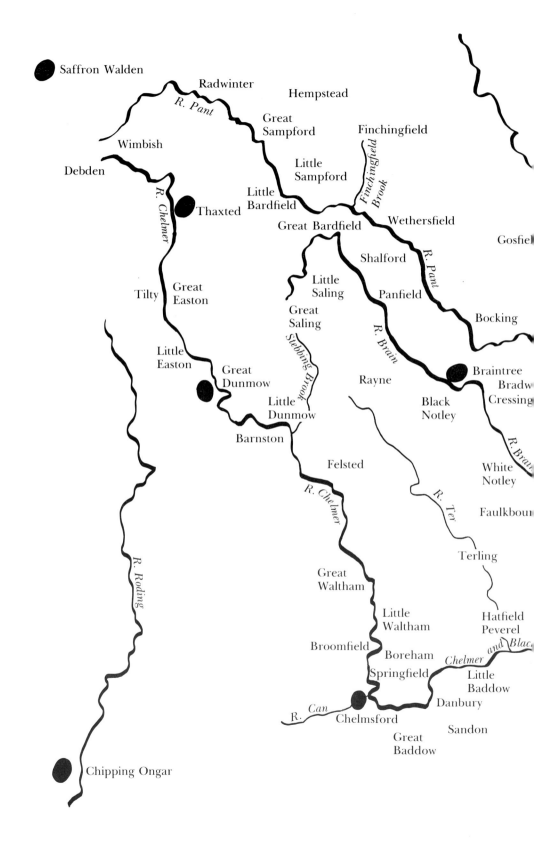

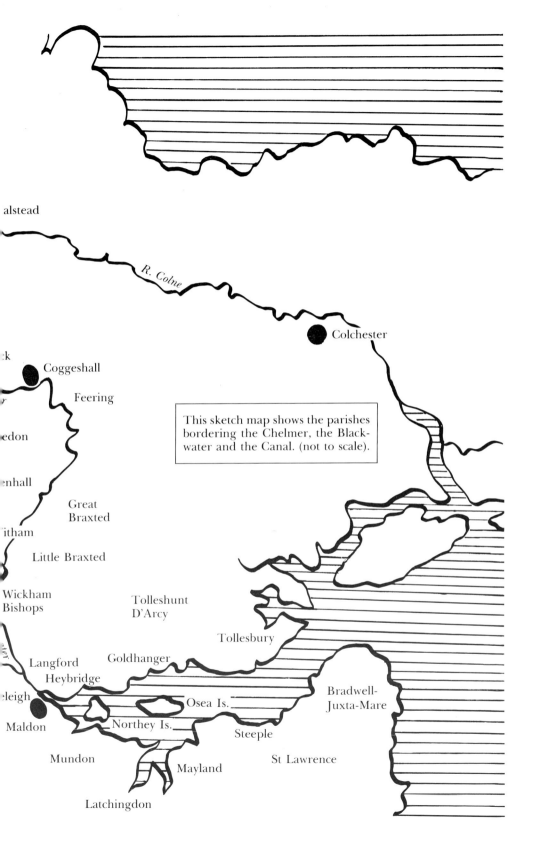

alstead

R. Colne

Colchester

Coggeshall

Feering

This sketch map shows the parishes bordering the Chelmer, the Blackwater and the Canal. (not to scale).

edon

k

r

nhall

Great Braxted

itham

Little Braxted

Wickham Bishops

Tolleshunt D'Arcy

Tollesbury

Langford

Goldhanger

Heybridge

eleigh

Osea Is.

Maldon

Northey Is.

Bradwell-Juxta-Mare

Steeple

Mundon

Mayland

St Lawrence

Latchingdon

CHAPTER ONE

The Chelmer—from Small Beginnings

I T IS simple enough for the expert to say that the Chelmer rises in Rowney Wood, half a mile south of Debden Airfield at a height of 370 feet above sea level, but it is no light proposition for the weekend walker to reach that particular spot. The way which appeared the best on the map to us was down the side road at Howlett End which leads to Pepples Farm. We knew we would be walking through history, for Reaney in his *Place-names of Essex* told us that a Robert Hulot gave his name to the hamlet in the middle of the thirteenth century and John Pypple, later written as Pimple, was farming there as early as 1434.

Beside an old, boarded-up cottage, once the home of a couple of families of farm labourers, the narrow lane petered out into a cart track running soggily between and below the fields. It twisted about for more than a mile before it delivered us at a point near enough to Rowney Wood to identify the Chelmer as a purling stream no more than a foot wide which had already carved a deep gully through the clay to a gravel bed. The track went on, invitingly, to Barnard's Farm and Debden Green but we had to forego that pleasure in following the course of the Chelmer towards Thaxted. The river starts its life in Debden, which Miller Christy, when encouraging cyclists to ride out and about with his *Handbook for Essex* in 1887, declared was "One of the most delightful parishes in the county, its surface being undulating and thickly wooded." That description still applies. The Hall, which he described as a "fine, large mansion, built in 1795, with porticoed, Grecian front," was designed by Henry Holland, son-in-law and pupil of "Capability" Brown and set in specially landscaped grounds, beside a large lake. Sadly it was destroyed by fire around 1920 and demolished in 1936. The servants' quarters, stables and other outbuildings have been transformed into an impressive private residence.

The church of St Mary the Virgin was built beside an older Hall on the same site in those early days when Saxon chiefs, converted to Christianity, had churches built close to their halls as much for their personal convenience as to

Left: The River Chelmer from Bowyer's Bridge, looking downstream.

afford the holy places their protection. St Mary's now benefits from the beautiful setting of Holland's Hall, all in isolated greenery where the lake glimmers through the trees. Within, it shows features of the thirteenth century in its arcade of pillars; the porch and windows in the south aisle are of the following century. The unusual feature is the chapel which the local magnate, Richard Chiswell, had specially designed by John Carter in 1793, in imitation of the typical chapterhouse of a monastery or cathedral. Chiswell died in 1797 and was laid to rest in his chapel, under a tomb chest beneath a richly decorated arch. He had also paid for a new font, completed in 1786 to Henry Holland's design, carried out in Coadestone—a wonderfully realistic simulation of real stone made at the Coade factory in Lambeth, the recipe for which is said to have been lost.

An interesting point about Debden is made by David Coller, writing in 1861:

It seems from the earliest ages to have been a favourite and fertile spot. At the time of the survey [ie Domesday], when it was in the possession of Ralph Peverell, it had four acres of vineyard, two of which were in bearing—a proof that the grape was then largely cultivated in the county, and the wine which cheered our forefathers was manufactured in their own homestead.

The old farm cottages on Pebble's Farm, Howlett End.

The Chelmer runs under its first road bridge near Proud's Farm.

It is pleasing to know that this ancient cultivation of the grape has been revived, on a commercial basis, at Felsted and at Purleigh.

The Chelmer runs away from Debden in an easterly direction towards the main road, the B184 north of Thaxted. This is the first road under which it passes, via a brick-arched bridge beside Prouds Farm; then it turns south in a great loop to cross under that road again at Armitage Bridge, which was widened by the United States Army in 1942. The name comes from the Armytage family of whom an Edward is mentioned in a local rental of 1592. It is by now more than a mere stream. Other unidentified headwaters have contributed their flow to the young river which runs briskly under the bridge.

Now the little Chelmer is in the parish of Thaxted, but, unlike the tourist, it shuns the attractions of that place, bending away to the west to skirt the town and bisect the lane between it and its hamlet of Cutlers Green. Cutlers Green is an unremarkable place today, one or two picturesque old houses, a couple of uncomfortably out-of-place, modern brick-and-glass confections, but it is worthy

3

of mention because its name is the very last, albeit prosaic, piece of surviving evidence that Thaxted was once a centre of the cutlery trade—the only one in the county and at the peak of its production in the fifteenth century. The vicar of Thaxted, the Reverend G. E. Symonds, writing in 1864, claimed that traces of forges had been found at Cutlers Green, and that oral tradition had it that houses had stood along the lane to Thaxted where the colony of cutlers had gathered. They formed a guild which included most of the crafts which worked metal, from the humble blacksmith to the gold beater. Without the vast amounts of wood needed for fuel or the water-power to stimulate increased production, it was inevitable that the cutlery craft should decline. That it was still practised into the seventeenth century was confirmed by the find of a farthing token issued by Nathaniel Smith. It bears the sign of two swords crossed, a sure indication that it came from a cutler.

The hall those cutlers built for their meeting-place still stands as the Thaxted Guildhall, photographed and admired by thousands of tourists. It has been restored sympathetically in recent times under the auspices of the County Council. Its all-timber construction with lath-and-plaster infilling is in the true tradition of medieval Essex building technique, using the materials they could find most readily to hand. The three-storeyed building, under a double-hipped roof, is open to the street on the ground floor, where no doubt objects of the cutlers' craft were displayed for sale. Guild meetings took place in the rooms above. When that trade declined cloth-working was introduced to maintain the town's prosperity. Those workers took over the Guildhall for their craft meetings. So it was saved for the present day, being used in the intervening period for all kinds of functions from a prison constructed on the ground floor to a meeting place for the town council above it.

For many a long year John Webb's mill had stood neglected, dejected. Then someone came forward to ask for volunteers to help in its restoration. Thaxted scouts worked hard at cleaning the mill generally and a committee set about raising funds. Up to the time of writing it has been a success story. The internal machinery has been restored or faithfully reproduced. The fantail has been repaired and now turns in the wind most attractively. The sails themselves could not be reclaimed from the rotting remains which lay for years in the nettles at the foot of the mill, but they will eventually be replaced. Then Thaxted will have a working monument to a local industry which involved so many crafts, from the farmer and the reaper to the miller and the baker. John Webb would be surprised to know that his mill is now on the tourists' itinerary because it has such an interesting collection of bygones gathered in and around the town and put on show on three floors. The climb up all those stairs is worth it, and what a bonus there is in the view from the top of the mill.

The jewel in Thaxted's crown is the church. Its spire marks Thaxted from afar—a spire which meant so much to one anonymous, home-coming inhabitant:

Majestic giant! lordly spire!
What joys thy aspect doth inspire,
When absent long from home and thee,
Thy towering beacon first I see!

Thy glittering vane (seen many a mile),
Proclaims my welcome with a smile;
And tells of home and evening fire,
Not far from thee, dear Thaxted Spire! . . .

The beauty of this church of St John the Baptist, so clear and light within, so complicated with pinnacles, battlements, gargoyles, buttresses, friezes and ornamentation outside, has to be seen; it cannot be adequately described. Standing quietly in the nave, one can hardly appreciate the noise, the shouting and jeering, the curses uttered and the blows exchanged on more than one occasion. Look back to that Friday, 24th September, 1647, when a great crowd of parishioners gathered here, determined that they would not have their minister compulsorily replaced. As Puritanism swept the country and civil war loomed, the minister of Thaxted, Newman Leader, was replaced at the order of the

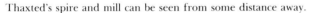

Thaxted's spire and mill can be seen from some distance away.

5

Committee for Plundered Ministers by a Mr Hall, reputed to be a godly, learned minister. Lady Maynard, who had the patronage of this appointment, would not agree to this, even though Newman Leader had died in the course of the negotiations. For some reason she favoured Edmund Croxon, despite the fact that he had already acquired a reputation as a drunken and dissolute blackguard. The parishioners were horrified. They protested to the Committee, which ordered Lady Maynard to make a new choice, thrice referring her to the people's preference for Mr Hall. That minister finally forced the issue by going to the church with a whole crowd of supporters, including the Mayor, and preaching the morning sermon. This was too much for the church officials, who in the afternoon barred his way to the pulpit. The incensed congregation set about them, beating them and tearing out handfuls of their hair, forcing them to flee the church in fear for their lives.

So seriously was this civil disobedience considered that the leading figures in this drama were taken before the House of Lords that very day. An astute London bookseller made a tidy profit by publishing a pamphlet entitled: "A Great Fight in the Church at Thaxted, Essex, Between the Sequestrators and the Minister . . ."

Such disgraceful scenes in the church were repeated in 1921. Conrad Noel, appointed vicar by a modern Maynard, Lady Warwick, served here for thirty-two years until his death in 1942. He was a strong socialist and as Lady Warwick herself had been attracted to the socialist cause, Noel's dual position as Secretary of the Church Socialist League and as grandson of the Earl of Gainsborough made him a most attractive candidate for the living of what she considered *her* church. Three hundred years on a Maynard lady was still influencing the direction of church affairs in Thaxted.

However, Conrad Noel went rather too far in his mixing of communism and Christianity in his church. Alongside the "old national flag of St George", as he put it, and the Sinn Fein flag given him by an Irish parishioner, he hoisted the red flag of revolution. Many of the townspeople were distressed by his action. Cambridge undergraduates came to hear of it. They descended on the church en masse, tore down his flags and put up the Union Jack. Noel's supporters ripped it down, burnt it, and replaced the offending flags. There was shouting and swearing in the church again on Empire Day when, quoting Noel again, ". . . one of my followers had his hat knocked off for refusing to remove it at the singing of *God Save the King*." The trouble spilled out into the street, with Noel and his friends slashing the tyres of cars and motor cycles parked in the Swan yard by the undergraduates.

It is strange to think that while Noel's "Battle of the Flags" was causing a national sensation, Gustav Holst was organizing the first music festival in Thaxted. He brought choirs and orchestras of national repute for which the grand old church made an appropriate setting. Holst told a friend: "It was a feast—an orgy. Four whole days of perpetual singing and playing."

This little town of Thaxted makes a mark on the memory not because of any buildings in particular, other than the church, but because it is a conglomeration of beautiful architecture, still in use as it was originally intended as houses, shops and meeting places.

From the middle of the town a road runs south-west towards Broxted over Dairy Green Bridge. A left turn at the fork, where the little Stan Brook runs under the road to make its contribution to the Chelmer, allows the motorist to follow the river valley by the narrowest of lanes which rises steeply then descends to Folly Mill Bridge over the Chelmer, rebuilt in 1942. Here the river has broadened in adolescence, running deep in the channel it has carved beside a house where the garden in spring is a carpet of snowdrops.

The last remains of Tilty Abbey.

It is necessary to return to the junction to pick up the road to Tilty, where a right turn brings into view the church of St Mary the Virgin and the minuscule remains of St Mary's Abbey in the great, green, sloping meadow. The Abbey was a Cistercian house—an order devoted to labour and industry in small, self-supporting communities of lay brethren. Just seven such brothers banded together to clear and drain this marshy site. That was in 1153. Their hard work was rewarded; more men joined them. The original rough buildings in wood and thatch were replaced by grander constructions in imported stone and rubble, together with bricks and tiles made from the brick-earth readily available on the banks of the Chelmer. In addition to their religious devotions, frequently made in strict obedience through day and night in their Abbey church, completed and consecrated in 1221, the brothers worked hard on the land. They kept sheep in vast flocks, harvesting their wool at annual shearings. Fine, white wool from Tilty was much sought after on the Continent; it was smuggled in large quantities to evade the tax placed upon its export to protect the Essex weavers against foreign competition. A leaflet available in the church today claims there are old Italian documents still in existence which prove that Tilty wool was sought even that far away.

The Abbey grew rich and plans were afoot for extension and adornment, but then came the dreaded plague, the Black Death, in 1349 and there were not enough survivors for the work to be put in hand. From then on the story of St Mary's Abbey is one of gradual decline down to its closure by Henry VIII in his dissolution of all monasteries from 1535. By 1542 its lands had passed to Thomas, Lord Audley of Walden, Lord Chancellor, born of lowly rank in Earls Colne in 1488. He had the buildings torn down and re-erected to form his own palatial residence. With the passing of the years that itself crumbled and was robbed of its stone and timber to build and repair houses over a wide area around it.

Tilty parish church and the restored east window.

The great feature still remaining is the parish church of St Mary, preserved simply because at the dissolution of the Abbey this little chapel at the gate to the Abbey grounds was granted to the villagers, who had always worshipped there, for use as their parish church. Its big east window, quite out of proportion with the present small building, is very beautiful in the unusual delicacy of its tracery. The porch, dated to the seventeenth century, is plastered in the manner known as pargeting, an ancient craft in Essex which raises figures and geometrical designs in relief in the wet plaster which protected old timber-framed buildings. It gave rise to the surname Pargeter. The architectural details are fully described by Pevsner in his Essex volume in the *Buildings of England* series.

The casual visitor will notice with interest the glass case containing finds made on the site of the Abbey all down the years—floor tiles, oyster shells, ancient glass, worked stones and jug handles. Worthless as individual items, they are an invaluable three-dimensional archive of the arts and crafts of builders and brothers alike.

Another point of interest is the window of clear glass set with coloured coats of arms subscribed with the explanation: "In praise of God these arms of original benefactors of Tilty Abbey were given by British home tobacco growers, AD 1952." This is the only clue the visitor has to an unusual experiment in agriculture in this parish, an experiment that illustrates that God does indeed move "in a mysterious way, His wonders to perform." It all started through the interest and personality of one man.

Hugh Cuthbertson, born in 1899 in Duxford, Cambridgeshire, grew up to be an aircraft draughtsman when the industry was in its infancy. He learned to fly, holding one of the early aviation licences. Then he met Conrad Noel, became interested in his "Thaxted Movement" within the Church of England and gave up his flying career to be trained for the Ministry. He and his wife Betty, married at Thaxted, worked enthusiastically in the emerging Socialist Clergy Movement. After exhausting work in poor parishes in London and Liverpool they took on a parish in Chile. They returned to England in 1934 and came to Tilty in 1939. Through the war they looked after evacuees to whom they gave up most of the vicarage.

Those years of war however had prevented the proper maintenance of the church; materials and labour just were not available. More than that, money for restoration of one humble village church among thousands pleading for help was very hard to come by. Hugh had an idea. When pipe tobacco became scarce he had experimented in growing his own. He was successful. He then let it be known in the parish magazine that he would pass on his tips for the best way to produce home-grown tobacco to anybody who would give five shillings towards the repair of Tilty tower. A newspaper spotted this item, made it known nationally, and the following morning Hugh had a sack left on his doorstep containing three hundred contributions, with more to follow. So this connection with tobacco, however much the habit of smoking is frowned upon today, was of direct and vital service to this ancient church.

Through Hugh's efforts the National Amateur Tobacco Growers' Association was formed in 1948. Though he left, giving the officers of the association a free hand in its development, they asked him to come back in 1951 because they needed his wise counsel. His advice led to the setting up, on 6th December of that year, of the Tilty Curing Co-operative which continues to this day. Hugh continued as vicar until 1962, when he took on another challenging dockland parish in London. But he and Betty had that affection for Tilty which brought them back here in retirement. Their daughter Cecile, a non-smoker, had taken her father's place in the tobacco co-operative while he was away. On his return they worked together, and were of tremendous service to those independent folk who grew their own tobacco but needed seeds, plants, the curing kiln and the expertise in all aspects of production which Hugh and Cecile passed on so generously.

Hugh Cuthbertson died in 1977, and once again his friends in the cultivation of that "tawney weed" gave thanks for the privilege of knowing him by contributing to a fund for restoring the east window, which was in danger of collapse. Cecile continues to edit *The Smoker*, the news sheet of the Tilty Tobacco Centre, and arranges curing of members' tobacco in the kiln constructed in the old church hall.

Standing by the church and looking out over the meadow where the Abbey once stood one can see in the left-hand corner of the field the ruins of a mill long since overtaken by modern developments in technology and trade. To the villagers this mill was the wonder of the age when it was built around 1750, probably at the same time as the church porch and the cottage next to it. The mill was not a totally new idea. It is quite likely that an old mill on the same site, a timber-framed building, had become so rickety that the brick walls were literally built round the framework and the machinery was overhauled.

Though the stream here is the merest trickle of a tributary to the Chelmer, it was specially widened and deepened with an embankment several hundred yards long to provide a sufficient head of water to drive the wheel. The wheel at that time was made of iron, fourteen feet in diameter, but the driving-shaft was solid timber of eighteen inches diameter, driving a great, wooden spur wheel eight feet across, connected to two pairs of millstones on the floor above. This is only a humble demonstration of the millwright's craft and of the great technical skill he needed to set up a water mill even from the earliest days. When the water failed in a summer drought the miller could not make a living. How pleased he

Right: Tilty Mill.

must have been when the newfangled steam engine allowed him to connect up to a third pair of stones, run independently by the engine installed beside the mill. The wheels and other iron fittings required to achieve this can still be seen on the walls.

Local mills like this were put totally out of production, made obsolete, by centralized production in large mills with easy access to road and rail and to ports into which so much foreign grain flowed. Long before the last war Tilty mill had ceased grinding. The farmer who owned it had the ingenuity to link the water-wheel to a hammer-mill, which processed his cattle food until 1957. Since then the mill has retreated into a wilderness of nettles and brambles, soon to become a picturesque ruin.

From Tilty, river and road keep company to the cross roads where Great Easton lies off to the east. The lane in that direction crosses the Chelmer by the unusual split-level Duton Hill Bridge. Pedestrians take the higher, arched bridge while wheeled traffic uses the lower, broader bridge, which has been known to be awash in times of flood.

The unusual split-level bridges over the Chelmer at Great Easton.

12

The river runs on past Butcher's Pasture, perhaps named after the famous Bourchier family which can be traced back to the fourteenth century in Essex, providing peers and politicians of national significance. The first Lord Bourchier, Robert, was much favoured by Edward III. His great-grandson, Henry, and his wife were buried at Beeleigh Abbey, but the memorial above their grave was moved to Little Easton by horse and cart when Beeleigh Abbey was dissolved by Henry VIII in 1536. Thus the chapel in the church at Little Easton was called the Bourchier Chapel, though more recently it has become known as the Maynard Chapel.

The Maynards owned the land for miles around, building on the industry and acumen of Sir Henry Maynard, founder of the Essex branch of this famous family, who had Little Easton Hall built to his order and died in 1610. His son was created the first Baron Maynard by James I in 1628, choosing the title Maynard of Estaines Parva, an ancient form of the name of Little Easton. He was Lord Lieutenant of Essex through troubled times from 1635 until his death in 1640. His splendid monument in that Maynard Chapel shows him in life-size effigy as a Roman commander. The Maynards continued loyal to the crown, suffered for it under Cromwell and were rewarded with the King's favour at the Restoration in 1660. The fifth Baron was made a Viscount in 1766. He died, unmarried, in 1775 and only the Viscountcy remained to succeeding generations. The third and last Viscount, son of the vicar of Thaxted, left his Easton estate to his granddaughter, Frances Evelyn Maynard, who became Countess of Warwick.

Little Easton is a peaceful place. The most exciting occurrence on a walk through the village was the opportunity to buy some fuchsias from a stall outside a house where the purchaser was asked to put the necessary coins into a tin. The old-time virtue of trust is still practised in deepest Essex. It could be said that Little Easton's times of fame and fun are behind it, for what could ever equal the days when the Prince of Wales came down to Easton Lodge, drawn by the beauty of Frances, Countess of Warwick, infatuated with the quickness of her mind, the gaiety of her companionship, the whirlwind of their courtship?

In 1929 Frances wrote her biography, called *Life's Ebb and Flow*. What a tide of memories it brings flooding in to older people round Dunmow way. Her connections with royalty and nobility were so intimate that, before publication of the book, "the hand of censorship touched it" and many interesting details had to be left out. Her grandfather died when she was three, in 1865, and he very unusually made her heir to his estate. Family feeling over this was so bitter that when they moved into the old family home at Easton Lodge she and her baby sister had a personal bodyguard to protect them against possible kidnapping.

It was planned by Lord Beaconsfield (Benjamin Disraeli) that she should marry Queen Victoria's youngest son, Prince Leopold, and to that end she was taken to a banquet at Windsor at which she was "quizzed" by the Queen.

Leopold, however, was already in love, secretly, with someone else and Frances herself fell in love with Lord Brooke, son of the Earl of Warwick. Her biography is studded with the names of well-known and important personalities:

> In town one can choose one's friends, but, in the country, neighbours, often uncongenial, are thrust upon us. My neighbours have been a constant delight and inspiration. My mind flies, above all, to my tenants at the Glebe, to H. G. Wells and his wife and all their interesting entourage. In my "Laundry" live Philip Guedalla and his beautiful wife (a type of the picture of "Rebecca at the Well"); at my Home Farm, Gustav and Isobel Holst have made a cottage into an abode of delight with an old barn for their music-room. Here their only child, Imogen, sends out the wonderful music that has gained her scholarships, at an early age, that men might envy. No more than a stone's throw from the Lodge the Horrabins rest from their editing of *Plebs* and their political canvassing of Peterborough. Near by the tall Marquis d'Oisy, image of a remote ancestor, the great Cardinal Richelieu, paints and decorates his furniture and composes pageants. In the old Easton Manor, where Edward IV and Elizabeth Woodville spent their protracted honeymoon, my youngest daughter Mercy, the wife of Basil Dean, entertains the stars of the theatrical profession at week-ends.

It was after she was married that she approached the Prince of Wales to appeal for help in the retrieval of an indiscreet letter. It was the start of a passionate liaison during which the Prince, in constant correspondence, addressed her in such terms as "my own lovely little Daisy wife." As a result of this affair Little Easton obtained its own station which was provided, somewhat reluctantly, by the railway company so that the Prince could go directly to his sweetheart's arms. She would meet him at the station with a wagonette and drive him herself back to the secrecy of that sanctuary at Easton Lodge where he could, as she said, perhaps a little tongue in cheek, "throw aside the heavy trappings of his state to revel in the love of nature."

After eight years the affair cooled when the Prince was attracted to a younger lady, Alice Keppel. It was then that Frances took the unusual step of becoming a committed socialist. She even opened the Chelmsford Star Co-operative Society's new buildings in 1902. Yet she continued to entertain on the grand scale, and fell into debt. Her money was not all wasted; she paid for a secondary school to be set up in Dunmow, an agricultural college solely for women, a hostel for women in Reading, a home for crippled children and a school of needlework for girls. By 1915 her financial position was desperate. She hit upon the idea of arranging to publish the Prince's letters to her on payment of £100,000 then, through an emissary, asked for that sum from King George V, on payment of which she would give him all the letters. The King's advisors acted swiftly and obtained a court order that the correspondence must be burnt forthwith in the envelopes which held it. Quietly her debts were paid by the emissary, who later received a knighthood.

Frances lived on at Easton Lodge after her husband died in 1924, still working where she could for the socialist cause, while the house became more and more neglected. She died in 1938, aged 77. Her monument, in Little Easton church, is a marble bust, showing her at the height of her beauty, simply inscribed: "Frances Evelyn Maynard, Countess of Warwick, Lady of the Manor of Estaines. Born December 10, 1861. Died July 26, 1938."

The road winds on to the A130 where the Chelmer meets with it at Bowyer's Bridge. Here the historians differed. One implied that Richard Bowyer, who was alive in 1489 when he was mentioned in national accounts now preserved in the Public Record Office, put in hand the building of this very important bridge. Another historian however provided quite different information for the plaque now fixed on the upstream parapet, which reads:

> To the glory of God and in grateful memory of Thomas Bowyer a weaver of Great Dunmow. He was burnt at the stake in Stratford-le-Bow on 27th June, 1556, aged 36 years for adherence to the Protestant faith . . . Provided by the Protestant Alliance, the Essex Protestant Council and the Dunmow Strict Baptist Church."

Bowyer's Bridge.

The bridge has been rebuilt, even realigned, several times in its long history and now dates from 1930. One of these rebuildings reminds us that here in the parish of Little Easton, actually on the Chelmer itself, was established the first mill whose wheel the gathering waters of the river were strong enough to turn. Its location is pinpointed on Chapman and André's Essex atlas for which surveys were made between 1772 and 1774, where it is noted as a corn mill. Kelly's Directory of Essex, 1933, named it as Elmbridge Mill and showed that John Stokes was the miller as well as being a farmer. He was the last miller, for in that same year the mill-wheel stopped turning for ever.

The origin of its name may be found in Wright's *History and Topography of the County of Essex*, published in 1835: "Little Easton lies northward of Great Dunmow, and the pleasant country village which belongs to it is on the border of the river Chelmer, over which it is approached by a wooden bridge . . .". There is no doubt that the bridge would have been made of long-lasting, rot-resisting elm. That brand new bridge drove Bowyer's name from local minds, and Elmbridge it became. It too in its turn has gone, and brick and steel bear loads undreamed of when the carpenter waded waist-deep in the water to fix his heavy timbers. The wooden bridge forgotten, the old name was resurrected and modern maps show it as Bowyer's Bridge.

While the river keeps at a discreet distance from Dunmow town it does run through its parish and close to its ancient church. That church, dedicated to the Virgin Mary, is known and loved by hundreds of inhabitants and visited and appreciated by thousands of tourists. The building which nobody liked to visit was the workhouse. Here, at Dunmow, was built a Union Workhouse, a vast place erected in 1840 through the joint contributions of twenty-five parishes in the neighbourhood. It made economic sense in that all those parish workhouses could be closed, saving costly upkeep and administration, for the central workhouse could accommodate five hundred people. It was sad though that those people, mostly the indigent old, were brought here from their villages as far away as Thaxted, and their relatives, worried about them, were quite unable to visit them in those days of the six-day working week and travel at the speed of the horse.

Rendered obsolete long before the First World War it was used to house German prisoners of war. Its subsequent history was a slow decline into ramshackle condition until, after the last war, it was bought and converted into a number of roomy flats. Owners can boast that they live in premises originally designed by the celebrated architect Sir Gilbert Scott at the vast cost, then, of ten thousand pounds. Surely, if ghosts do walk, these flat-dwellers have felt the presence of those sad and sorry folk, segregated by sex, sent away from family and friends, awaiting the ultimate release from poverty and pain.

From the Union House we return to the river and its bridges. South of the church, the B1057 Stebbing road crosses the Chelmer over a bridge which was

The church at Dunmow, dedicated to the Virgin Mary.

The old union workhouse at Dunmow.

rebuilt and reopened with some pomp and ceremony on 7th June, 1882, a day of brilliant sunshine in a cloudless sky. Lord and Lady Brooke (better known later as Frances, Countess of Warwick) made their first public appearance after returning from their honeymoon. Amidst the fluttering pennants the band of the 2nd Essex Rifle Volunteers played suitable airs and marches. Then Lady Brooke was invited to formally place the last stone in position, to the applause of some three thousand enthusiastic inhabitants.

Three-quarters of a mile downstream the old A120, the Stane Street, crosses the Chelmer and heads east to Braintree. When the Romans built that road they used the shallowest part of the river they could find, built their ford and then bent their road from its ramrod straightness to make the connection. The Saxons were so impressed by this highway with its graded gravel surface that they called it the stone street, and "Stane Street" it remained right down to the day when all our roads were given impersonal classification by letter and number. Though a bridge was built early on the ford stayed in use for more than one reason. In the days when cattle, sheep and pigs were walked to market the ford was an important watering hole on the way. A hundred years ago, in the age of steam, Gargantuan traction engines were produced which could break a bridge with their weight, but they trundled through the ford and up the gentle rise with ease. Since the new bridge just a little further downstream now takes much of the traffic round the Dunmow bypass, the new A120, this bridge and this part of Braintree Road, as it is known in Dunmow, is altogether more peaceful. A small picnic area had been provided upstream of the bridge, with benches and tables and parking space for cars.

Where the Chelmer bears away east it forms the boundary between Little Dunmow and Barnston. It was in Little Dunmow that the ancient custom of the Dunmow Flitch originated.

It took the form of a trial, quite simple in itself; if a couple, interviewed separately by a jury of priors, could convince them that they had lived in married bliss without a single cross word for a year and a day they were awarded a flitch, or side, of bacon. Afterwards, ensconced in special chairs fitted with shafts, they were carried aloft through the village in triumphal procession.

The practice was introduced by the founder of Little Dunmow Priory so long ago that the date has been quite lost.

Since the Priory was founded in 1104 by the wife or the sister of Ralph Baynard, it was probably she who charged the priors from the outset with the provision of the flitch. At that time it could only have been a woman who would have encouraged faithfulness by example and marital harmony in a manner which would appeal to the common folk, and a side of bacon meant far more to a family than a new car would today as a prize in a national contest.

It was a nationally known custom by the fourteenth century. Geoffrey Chaucer mentions it in the *Canterbury Tales*—the one told by the Wife of

The peaceful picnic area at Dunmow.

Bath—and that was being written around 1387:

> The bacoun was nat fet for hem, I trowe,
> That som men han in Essex at Dunmowe.

The church of St Mary was originally the little Lady Chapel of the huge Priory church, so we can stand where those priors stood when that first noisy, cheerful yet quite serious trial took place. In the chancel of St Mary's there still stands a chair, complete with holes to take long shafts, which is said to be one of the original chairs used in the trial, but modern opinion is that, though the timber might be old enough and reused, its construction suggests it was made for a later revival of the old ceremony.

The earliest winners on record are Richard Wright and his wife who, even in the difficult days of travel in 1444, came all the way from Bradborn in Norfolk to claim the flitch. The custom fell into abeyance when the Priory was closed by Henry VIII, though responsibility for the provision of the bacon was passed to the Lord of the Manor. In 1751 the flitch trials were revived by the Lord of the Manor, and it is from this pattern that today's light-hearted entertainment is copied. A hundred years later the famous novelist Harrison Ainsworth was so taken with the idea that he paid for a couple of flitches himself so that the custom could once again be practised. In modern times the trials have been reintroduced, moving into the parish of Great Dunmow, but the old intention of encouraging constancy and loving tolerance is lost in the fun and games, particularly when television personalities make up the jury and the American Air Force puts on a flying display, as happened in 1988. One of the winning couples of a flitch then was Russell Green, a former Mayor of Saffron Walden, and his wife Marion. They went home with the bacon and the blessing summed up in the old poem:

> For this is our custom at Dunmow well known;
> Tho' the pleasure be ours, the bacon's your own.

19

CHAPTER TWO

The Chelmer Meets the County Town

THE CHELMER seems shy of making the acquaintance of Felsted. It meanders into the parish but does not approach the village. Here it receives the contribution of the Stebbing Brook, close by the lagoons of the Felsted sugar factory. The Felsted Sugar Beet Factory, to give it its full name, was registered in October, 1925. It was pioneered by the Second Anglo-Scottish Beet Sugar Corporation Ltd and was built on a greenfield site immediately north of the river in a corner made by the railway, which was then a vital part of the plan, and the road as it runs south and east to the village centre. Today the factory has a dejected air. The lawns are mown, but the gardens are overgrown and weeds have invaded the carpark. The official term for the state of the factory at the time of writing is "non-productive". The big silos, a landmark in a rural landscape, are now used to store sugar brought by tankers from active factories, preparatory to distribution to sweet manufacturers, soft drinks merchants, jam-makers and other bulk users. In just over sixty years the sugar industry in Essex has risen, flourished and died. It started amidst some controversy, as shown in the local newspaper of 19th February, 1926:

> In the House of Commons on Tuesday, Mr Duncan said the Minister of Labour did not seem to be aware of the fact that the following notice was displayed at the sugar-beet factory at Felsted: "No agricultural worker applying will be started. Anyone starting and found to be a land worker will be instantly dismissed." There seemed to be a conspiracy, connived at, he thought, by the Minister, between Labour Exchange and the farmers to prevent agricultural workers from getting employment at higher wages in these factories.

Put this quote beside the following advertisement appearing in the same issue of the paper:

> FARMERS – You are cordially invited to bring your Friends to see a FILM showing the life-history of Beet Sugar from the Seed to the Breakfast Table . . . GROW SUGAR-BEET for the All-British Felsted Factory.

and it is clear that the factory needed the farmers so much for the essential supply of sugar-beet that they had to walk a tightrope between obtaining

Left: Felsted sugar factory.

sufficient local labour by offering a competitive wage and offending the farmers by making their labourers look for an increase in *their* wages.

Felsted parish church is dedicated to the Holy Cross. It is, by and large, a much restored building of the fourteenth century, keyed into the stout Norman tower under an eighteenth-century cupola. The interior, however, reveals structures, pillars and doorways introduced through the years, which separate the tower and its cupola. The church has been the community centre for Felsted people for all that time and still offers peace, hope and friendship to all.

The Easter Sepulchre in the chancel dates from around 1350. In those early days the Church celebrated Easter with a special ceremony, re-enacting the laying of Christ's body in the tomb. An effigy of Christ was placed on top of a tombchest in a recess made in the wall of the chancel near the altar, the holiest part of the church. The ceremony had such an important place in the calendar of Christian worship that the sepulchre was as beautifully carved as the artist could execute and the community could afford. The Easter Sepulchre at Felsted though is not quite what it seems. An expert has researched the matter thoroughly and shown that the tombchest at present within this recess has been moved in former times from the east end of the south aisle.

The grandest monument in the church provides the link between the church and the famous Felsted School. It is the memorial to Richard Rich. He was born in 1500, was Solicitor-General in 1533, Speaker of the House of Commons in 1537, and in 1548 was appointed Lord Chancellor. He founded the school in 1564, and the original schoolhouse, still standing though no longer used for the purpose, was the schoolmaster's little kingdom down to 1866.

South of the river the A130 runs south-east through Barnston. The river skirts the village as it flows on to form the boundary between Felsted and Great Waltham, but Barnston is worth a visit for more than one reason. Places like Wellstye Green, Albanes and Bickners Farm reflect the names of families living here in the thirteenth and fourteenth centuries. The church must be the focal point.

It retains much of its Norman construction, clearly visible in the big round doorway, but the chancel, with its window architecture in the Early English style, was rebuilt in the thirteenth century. Later features include the tiny weather-boarded belfry put up in the fifteenth century and crowned three hundred years later with the pretty cupola. It is a typical Essex village church, repaired and extended in reverence and in piety by the efforts of the villagers for nearly a thousand years.

The river runs on eastward, with the parish of Great Waltham pointing a long finger to its southern bank to divide Barnston from Felsted. Causeway End, the hamlet to the south of Felsted, reminds us of the proximity of the river and of the winter flooding which necessitated a causeway, or raised road, to be constructed to keep communication with the hamlet through the worst weather.

Here, on the left and looking downstream, stands Felsted Mill.

A mill on this site was recorded in the Domesday Book. In 1373 it was mentioned as belonging to Leighs Priory. In 1427 it was named specifically as a corn mill. On early maps it was shown as Abchill or Abchild Mill but in 1850 the Ordnance Survey gave it the practical and sensible name of Felsted Mill. Just prior to that date it had been worked by Robert Dixon, but by 1848 William Ridley was there, a member of the well-known milling, malting and brewing family. He it was who had to cope with the burning down of the mill in about 1857. It was rebuilt by C. Livermore in 1858, confirmed by the date inscribed on the small chimney stack of the present four-storeyed brick building. It was still working up to about thirty years ago, but now only the mill-house shows signs of life.

Felsted Mill.

Freed from the restraint of the mill-wheel the Chelmer froths through the millrace and meanders southward, going under the road to North End at Absol Bridge, which was widened in 1929. Its name is a reminder of the big Abfield or Abchild Park estate acquired from the Duke of Suffolk by Lord Rich in 1538.

23

The bridge between Felsted and North End.

The river turns east between Felsted and Great Waltham, whimsically it may seem, but in reality it is following the contours of the countryside. Before we follow it further we must digress to the A130 where it is joined by the lane from North End, because here, on the very edge of the parish of Great Waltham, stands the Black Chapel, looking exactly the same as it did in 1768 when Philip Morant, an historian, wrote:

> In North-end, by the side of the road leading . . . to Dunmow, stands a little timber building, with a wooden turret, called Black Chapel, being a Chapel of Ease for this distant part of the parish: but they are obliged to bury their dead in Waltham church-yard. A lady of the Wiseman family, seated at Bullocks, left a farm near this chapel, for the endowment of it . . . The Vicar, it is said, is excepted from being preacher here, that he may not be induced to neglect the mother-church.

It is thought that the adjective "Black" is derived from the Blacche family which was influential hereabouts in the thirteenth and fourteenth centuries.

Where the river meets the road, the B1417, at Hartford End, Felsted's outlying hamlet, there is another mill just up river from Ridley's Brewery. The Ridley family had been operating it at least as far back as 1839, and it continued in production until 1919 or thereabouts. The mill closed finally in 1923, having been used only as a provender mill from the onset of the First World War. Its

Hartford End Mill (August 1933).

machinery, much of it wooden, mouldered away. There was neither time nor material available during the Second World War to stop the rot, so afterwards all the machinery and equipment was stripped out. It once had the unusual feature of a thatched roof but that had to be replaced with a tiled mansard-roof. Now the eighteenth-century, timber-framed and boarded mill together with the miller's house which adjoins it has been converted into a very peaceful and charming family residence.

Ridley's beer, brewed here at the Hartford End Brewery, is popular far beyond the boundaries of the county. The brewery, built in 1842, had been described as "one of the most picturesque 'tower' breweries remaining in operation in England", but it is so tucked away that one has to approach within a quarter of a mile from any direction before seeing it. It was built for Thomas Dixon Ridley, eldest son of William Ridley, the miller, who lived in the Mill House. Thomas saw the advantages to be gained from adding the brewing business to the traditional family undertaking of milling and malting. The brewery was sited close to road and river, the former for transport of raw materials and the product, the latter for its value as a drain in the course of the brewing process. The water supply to the brewery was from the natural springs on the hills around. It was not long before this man, very modern in his outlook

The Brewery at Hartford End.

and a steam-power enthusiast, installed a steam engine, known from the first thrust of its piston as "Lydia" to everybody in the brewery.

The two businesses carried on independently until 1906, when both enterprises were united in a single, limited company by the chairman, Charles Ernest Ridley. By that time the company had acquired forty-seven public houses. Its success continued, and by 1988 the brewery owned sixty-five houses and supplied beer to other tied and free houses. The company still thrives in the hands of the descendants of the founder, and a younger generation waits in the wings to carry on this fine performance. Herbert Knight, an old employee, writing of his memories of the nineteen-thirties onwards, concludes: "It was due to the war that the river was neglected and floods were very common and often the lawn at the back of the Mill House became flooded and water went in one side of the house and out of the other. On one occasion the bridge at the Mill House was washed away including the roadway as well. This was about 1948 and with Mr Gerald Ridley insisting that the line of the old bridge be followed, the overhang you can now see is the result; at this time the wheel was taken out of the mill and other machinery was dismantled."

From the Brewery the river runs under the road, turns south again and passes by Littley Green, the "Little Enclosure" as it was called by the first settlers who cleared and cultivated the old forest in Saxon times. Now the Chelmer is in the parish of Great Waltham, running parallel with the main road and "back road" until all three meet the A131 at Little Waltham. On the way the Chelmer slides past the mill house at Howe Street. Now a private house, it was restored just before the last war and stands in beautiful gardens, which are sometimes opened to the public in aid of charity. The waterfall nearby marks the site of the mill-wheel. The big clapboard mill itself, first mentioned in a court-roll of 1400, was last manned by James Martin before the First World War, and then demolished in 1928.

While the river waters Langleys in its pleasant park, let us touch on the story of this large parish of Great Waltham. Its first settlers were those people who had acquired the knowledge of the use of iron. With their crude axes they hacked out a place of settlement from forest and scrub down by the river where the Little Waltham bypass now runs. This Iron Age tribe lived as wastefully of nature's resources as do the gypsies we sometimes see parked on grass verges in the parish today. Theirs was a continuous battle for survival against natural hazards which needed total tribal self-sufficiency. The advent of the Romans must have come as the greatest of shocks to them. From settlement to settlement the message had been passed on, from Kent through Essex, that a highly disciplined and well-armed enemy was on its way to capture Colchester and bring to heel the two sons of King Cunobelin who, unlike their late father, refused to be vassals of Rome. The straight road from Little Waltham to Braintree is lasting evidence of the presence of Romans in this area. Whether they recruited the local British into their road-making gangs, we shall never know.

What did the Romans leave behind to remind us of their four hundred years' stay? Very little in present-day Great Waltham—but a great deal at Ashtree Corner nearer the river. One item found which brings those Romano-British very close is a leather sandal with a broken strap, perfectly preserved in the peaty sediment at the bottom of a Roman well. Perhaps some tired traveller, resting and refreshing himself at the well, found that broken strap the last straw, so he pitched the sandal down the well in disgust and hobbled off to the village for a new pair.

Then came the Saxons who gave the place its name, practical enough, of the "settlement in the forest"—Waltham, which as the population grew, split into the

27

The Mill House at Hare Street.

Great and Little parishes. Langleys is not old in the history of the place, though the estate can be traced back to ownership by the Marshall family at the beginning of the thirteenth century when King John was on the throne. The well-known family which lived here from 1515 was the Everards. The estate then included "one messuage, a water-mill, 140 acres of arable, 12 of meadow, 52 of pasture", all at a rent of 46s and 3 capons per annum. In the sixteenth century

The mill stream at Hare Street.

Richard Everard married Clementia Wiseman of the important Great Canfield family. The next Richard was made a Baronet in 1628, and the Everards proudly walked about their gardens on the banks of the Chelmer, but within the next eighty years the family had squandered all their inheritance and the Sir Richard Everard of the next generation had to sell off the estate to pay his debts.

The next owner, Samuel Tufnell, saw it as a very pleasant place to live, near enough to the capital to allow him to attend to his business affairs, but far enough away to escape the risks of disease, robbery and foul air of the "wen of London". He had most of the old mansion pulled down in about 1718 and built a new house to his own design. He also planned the park in which it still stands. He died in 1758 but it has remained in his family ever since. Cameras are not allowed closer than the drive, from which there is a beautiful view of the house but the well-known Chelmsford photographer, Frederick Spalding, was allowed in the house at the turn of the century to take photographs. The lower and upper rooms in the north wing attract most attention in books on architecture because of the richness of the decoration on their plaster ceilings and their intricately carved fireplaces. Pevsner thought these rooms displayed "plaster-work of an exuberance not exceeded anywhere in the country." Other rooms show ornamentation of about 1800; the White Room is one of them. The furniture in it was specially designed by Charles Elliott, furnisher to His Majesty King George III between 1784 and 1810.

29

In the centre of the village an insignificant piece of piping rising up from the pavement is the relic of Great Waltham's very ingenious first piped water supply. The *Parish Magazine* reported in 1889:

> The spring in Bury Meads opposite Mr Lucking's [the butcher's] has supplied nearly the whole village with drinking water. We need not say at what inconvenience water has been fetched, in all weathers, from the further ends of the village. Happily we can see our way to a better provision for the future. A committee of villagers worked out this scheme: the water from a spring in South House Meadows will be forced by an hydraulic ram into a tank placed in a raised position close to the stile leading to Mr Pyne's pasture in South Street. Water would be conveyed from it by pipes to the schools, the Club Room and three points in the village, one at the top of South Street, another near Messrs Bigg's bakery and third opposite the Vicarage gate at the entrance of Barrack Lane.

By February, 1890, it was further reported in the *Parish Magazine*: "This important undertaking has now got into fair working order. Frost and various other unlooked-for difficulties caused considerable delay. The ingenious little machine at the spring head does its work satisfactorily and throws an ample supply into the tank . . . it will take a little time before the water is entirely free from the taste of the new pipes." The *1937 Directory* still reports: "Water is supplied from three public hydrants in the village."

The village inn, the Six Bells, is adorned with pargeting, but the work is modern, done by one of the last exponents of the craft, Fred Willett of Chelmsford.

The Church of St Mary and St Lawrence reveals much of the history of the village; its walls, six centuries old, were buttressed two hundred years ago with bricks made in the parish. On the Everard tomb, set up in 1611, Sir Anthony Everard and his wife lie stiffly in full-size effigy on shelves, with their children represented by miniature figures on tombchests. The Wyseman family is remembered by a brass made about 1580 showing Thomas Wyseman and one of his wives beautifully portrayed in the costume of the time; the brass has been defaced and the figures of his other wife and daughters destroyed, while those of his sons can still be deciphered, together with the solemn epitaph:

> Who lyste to see & know himself
> May loke upon this glasse
> And wey the beaten paths of Death
> Which he shall one day pass
> Which way Thomas Wyseman
> With patient mynde hath gonne.
> Whose Bodye here as Death hath charged
> Lyeth covered with this stonne
> Thus Dust to Dust is brought againe
> The earth she hath her owne
> This shall the lott of all men be
> Befoore the Trump be blowen.

A very famous man of Essex is connected with this church. Philip Morant, born in Jersey, was curate here for eight years from 1724. He can truly be called a man of Essex because he wrote the first complete history of Essex, which came out in parts between 1760 and 1768. It can be seen in most libraries in the recent reprint. Over seven pages are devoted to this relatively small village of Great Waltham. Could it be that Morant treated it so fully out of sheer affection? Of the manor house at Walthambury he said: "The mansion-house stands near a mile west-north-west from the church, and is but mean," but of the estate he concludes: "This is a noble maner; the lands and demesnes belonging to it containing no less than 800 acres."

The Chelmer, indifferent to history and the doings of mere man, meanders on past Minnows End into the parish of Little Waltham, neatly summed up by an historian, writing in 1861, as "a village on the Braintree road, with well-timbered hills, and lands pleasantly sloping to the river, over which the county built a neat bridge seven years ago." Winckford Bridge traces its name back to 1194 as Winckeford—evidence of its importance as a river crossing long before the bridge was built. It has been widened, realigned and strengthened in 1954, 1969 and 1973. Its repair and upkeep have been the subject of village meetings and court proceedings through more than six hundred years.

In 1351, when the rough timber bridge had broken through much use and little maintenance, the village elders of Broomfield, Great Waltham, Little Waltham and Great Leighs trooped into court at Chelmsford to declare that the

Winckford Bridge at Little Waltham.

money had always been found in the past from the donations of benefactors, and not from what we would call today the "rates". The judge wisely declared that since the bridge was a distinct advantage to the villagers they would have to pay for its urgent repairs, with Great Waltham paying one half and the other half shared by the three smaller parishes.

A water-mill once stood just downstream of the bridge but nothing is left of it now. Those remains on the site, a broken concrete tower and a sluice, are the later relics of a water-driven dynamo, installed just before the war to supply power and light for the dog-racing track set up behind the present Waltham Service Station.

Little Waltham has a recorded history going back before Domesday, but the story we like is of the village Home Guard in the Second World War. Those valiant men of older age worked hard all day to make up for the absence of the younger men in the services, then they turned out again at night and on Sundays to keep in trim as a fighting force lest their village was invaded. An exercise was arranged one evening. A military "inspector" came down to put them through their paces. The police and the ARP were brought into the action. The inspector postulated the dropping of two bombs behind the barn at the top of The Street and set his stop-watch. The Home Guard commander briefed his officers, who briefed their sergeants, one of whom sent two men to investigate and report. Twenty minutes passed, the inspector got agitated, the commander got irritated and the sergeant got exasperated. He set off to find the men. They were nowhere near the barn. Knowing them well he went to one of their homes and found them both sitting down to supper in the kitchen. The sergeant was amazed and asked why they had not reported. "Lor' bless you," was the reply, "we went there, but there weren't no bombs at all, so we come on home!"

The river has entered Broomfield and runs under Croxtons Mill, so called from at least the middle of the eighteenth century. The white clapboard, timber-framed mill makes a most pleasing contrast with the green trees grouped about it, especially when viewed from the A130, the Broomfield road. For many years it had been worked by the Marriage family. After the death of Henry Marriage in December, 1938, and on the disposal of his estate, the mill was sold on 17th July, 1942, together with the cottages nearby, for £305. In 1988 the mill alone, transformed into a private residence, was inviting "offers in excess of £400,000."

Some memories of the mill when it was at work have been set down in Marriage's anniversary booklet, "*150 Years of Milling and Farming*", including:

Right: The attractive timber-framed Croxton's Mill.

Croxton's Mill and cottages in the distance provide a delightful view.

Croxtons Mill was the mill highest up the Chelmer to be owned and worked by the Marriage family. They also owned the adjoining meadow. So the farm men and the mill staff combined to make the hay, load it, and cart it through the ford which had a 'trick' turn in the middle which had to be known or the horses could well find themselves out of their depth . . . This Mill, all timber-built, had to be "loaded" correctly as to the weight in the Bins and on the Floors, or else the whole structure would lean dangerously sideways. Not only did this put the building at risk, it also opened the floor boards and allowed the grain to pour out into the river!

In those days before the war the Marriage children were taken regularly to Croxtons Mill where they were weighed on the mill scales to see that they were continuing in normal healthy growth.

Both Broomfield and Springfield are old villages whose quiet development was hustled and hastened by the happenings in the up-and-coming county town from the beginning of the century. Now it is not possible to see where Chelmsford ends and Broomfield begins, but up by the church of St Mary there is still the chance to experience the peace of the old village of Broomfield. The Normans put their Saxon vassals to work in the building of the church with its unusual round tower. The pretty, shingled spire above it is later, but the nave and the chancel are surviving Norman work, in which many a Roman brick and tile can be detected. However, Broomfield can claim a very much older connection with the past, the burial of a great Saxon chieftain.

In 1894 men were digging out gravel for farmer David Christy in a gravel pit "just behind Clobb's Row". They came across parts of a sword, a spear, a knife and other remains about six feet down, and thought no more of it! Six years later when gravel was worked from the same pit the diggers came across a grave partly cut away in that earlier excavation. The presence of those weapons was explained, and further finds included fragments of a bronze pan, two sapphire-

34

coloured glass vases and two wooden cups with rims of gilt bronze. What this group represented remains a mystery and other finds only add to the enigma. For example, two buckets made of wood, with iron mounts, had been sunk in the earth nearby so that their rims were level with the floor of the grave. There was also a strange iron cup shaped like half a coconut on a four-footed leg, a unique feature in Saxon graves so far excavated. It seems that the body of some Saxon chief had been placed in a coffin and burnt to ashes as it lay in the ground. It must have smouldered away very gradually, for the heat did not affect the glass and wooden vessels or the fabulous gold bracelet and rings which have survived in excellent condition. All these finds, which give Broomfield an important place in the annals of archaeology, were presented by Mr Christy to the British Museum, and some can be seen on display there.

The Domesday Book of 1086 shows that there was only enough woodland to support just one pig, indicating therefore that there was plenty of meadow, and enough corn was already being grown in Saxon times to make a watermill necessary. That mill is a strong thread in the tapestry of the Broomfield story. At a later date a windmill was built nearby. It is remembered in the "Windmill Pasture", home of one of the Marriage family of millers on the Chelmer through more than two hundred years. The water-mill was sited down the lane which is still called Mill Lane. Though it was demolished in 1919 the miller's house stands there today. What that mill meant to the villagers can hardly be appreciated today. Bread truly was their staff of life, especially when winter months made vegetables scarce and meat a luxury. The flour from the mill became a vital necessity.

The men who made milling a profitable business here early in the nineteenth century were the Marriage twins, William and Henry. From 1824 they built up the great milling and farming business which continues as a family concern today. They had the acumen to install a steam-engine as early as 1836, but they had to place it on the other bank of the river, opposite the mill itself. This certainly reduced the risk of fire, but it meant that long, strong driving belts had to leave the engine-house high in the air to cross the river and drive the stones in the mill. The plaque put up to celebrate this innovation has been incorporated in the present modern mill off New Street in Chelmsford.

Subsequent generations of Marriages took to growing what they ground; today there are farms all around which carry on the family business. Woolpits, Gardeners and Parsonage Farms are some of them, but the one most worthy of mention is Partridge Green Farm. It has passed out of the family except for the tiniest piece of land the size of a grave—and that is what it is, the tomb of Ruth Marriage. She married William in 1721. When he died in 1738 she carried on managing the farm for another thirty-four years. She was of the Quaker faith. When she died she was simply and reverently buried in her orchard. Though the fruit trees have long since been grubbed out, a lone crab-apple shades the grave whose sanctity has been honoured down to this day.

The Chelmer winds in a wide flood valley, crossed in very recent times by the two bridges of the new roads which are part of Chelmsford's plan to relieve the town centre of the increasing volume of traffic generated by the rapid development of industrial and residential estates. The satellite villages of Broomfield, Springfield, Sandon, Great Baddow, Galleywood and Writtle have all suffered an identity crisis to a greater or lesser degree. The new road system has altered the landscape in the same way as the railway did when it was pushed out from London to Colchester in 1845. Across the vales of the Chelmer and the Can viaducts had to be built.

Travellers through Chelmsford see the railway viaduct as a necessary adjunct to the line pioneered by the Eastern Counties Railway Company in 1843. Citizens see the brick piers and high arches striding across park, river and road as something of a blot on the landscape, but at last the sheer daring and brilliant engineering of those railway designers is being recognised, and stations, bridges and viaducts are being seen as examples of industrial archaeology, to be preserved for the insight they give us into that great age of steam.

When one considers the oozing, yielding clay of the meadows where Can and Chelmer flow it is something of a miracle that the viaduct has stood firm, with its feet sometimes in the very river itself, through nearly one hundred and fifty years. The weight of the trains which have crossed it in that time cannot be imagined, and the floods which have battered its buttresses in winter storms cannot be counted. When it was built the architect made it as graceful as he could with the material he was forced to use—bricks. Stone was out of the question owing to the cost of transport from distant quarries, and ferro-concrete had not yet been invented. Bricks by the thousand could be made on the spot from the brick-earth alongside the rivers, supplemented from the many other brickfields in the county.

The *Essex Chronicle* of 3rd March, 1843, tells of the first test trip along the railway line by the twenty directors, designers and engineers as it approached Chelmsford:

> After emerging from the cutting, a prominent feature of the works, the Can viaduct presented itself—as fine a specimen of a work of the kind as is to be found upon any line in the kingdom. It consists of 18 arches, each of them of 30 feet span, and 44 feet in height, with massive wings to sustain the embankment at each end. Topped with a light and elegant iron parapet, which is now in the course of erection it forms a beautiful and picturesque object when viewed from New London Road. A short embankment connects this with the Chelmsford viaduct, and in the erection of the two structures 10,400,000 bricks have been laid.
>
> The Chelmsford viaduct is a master-piece in this department of railway works. The construction is of a peculiar nature, being a double line of arches, extending upwards of 800 feet, the stone approaches to the station passing between them. Thus the down line is on one side and the up line on the other; and the advantage of this arrangement will be evident when it is stated that the object is to prevent the necessity

for any passenger crossing the line and exposing himself to the chance of accidents. The station, as we have before stated, is a neat, elegant and light structure of timber, in which every accommodation is afforded for the public and the officers.

We take travel by train so much for granted today that it is difficult to appreciate the great excitement occasioned by that first journey, summed up quaintly to the modern ear by the reporter on the spot:

> About half past twelve o'clock the shrill whistle of the fiery visitant, and the rumble of the train which he bore so steadily up to the station, turned many a wondering eye in Chelmsford in that direction, and soon parties began to trip thitherward, to the desertion of the fireside or shop, and the emptying of "mine Host's" inviting benches, to indulge in a little speculative curiosity on the snorting stranger.

Chelmsford's history from ancient times is being written by Hilda Grieve, the well-known archivist and historian, in her retirement. At least one volume is now available. Let us, therefore, look only at those features immediately related to the Chelmer. Passing under the railway, the river passes the site, off Rectory Lane, of Bishop's Hall Mill. As the name indicates it was once owned by the Bishop of London. All the land on which Chelmsford stood was given to the church even before the Domesday record of 1086. The mill was leased for centuries to local millers like John Markdaye, who was there in 1514. In 1563 the mill, along with all the Chelmsford property, came into the possession of the Mildmay family. It is possible that during their tenure the mill was rented for a period by the Strutt family, whom we shall meet again at Springfield Mill. A rental record of 1795 names Joseph Marriage as lessee of Bishop's Hall Mill for nineteen years at thirty-five pounds per annum.

That family continued there until 1914, to be followed by the Lings, another family known in Chelmsford as grain and feed merchants into very recent times. When it was sold by the Mildmays in 1917 the catalogue said it was "erected of brick and timber with a tiled roof. It is on four floors and is fitted with an undershot water wheel . . . the whole property is let to G. B. Ling . . .". This tangible piece of history was lost when the mill was burned down in a disastrous fire in 1930. As every Chelmsfordian knows, the site was taken over by the Hoffmann Manufacturing Co. Ltd, producers of ball-bearings, who used the surviving eighteenth-century miller's house as the chairman's dining room. From the midst of that massive factory complex the river still runs through the old millrace to find a brief freedom before being harnessed once again in the service of man at Springfield Mill, beyond the railway viaduct.

The white, weather-boarded mill, on the very edge of Victoria Road where it passes over the Chelmer, and its neat, brick, miller's house of Georgian origin make a vivid impression in the rather drab urban scene. For ninety years, from 1690, it was owned by the Strutts. One of the family achieved fame far greater than a local reputation as a wealthy miller. He was Joseph Strutt, born in 1749 to Thomas and his wife Elizabeth, the daughter of John Ingold, the miller at

Woodham Walter. He started life in this very mill, but he was hardly more than a year old when his father died. This did not prevent him from attending King Edward's School in Chelmsford until he was fourteen, when he was apprenticed to the engraver, William Ryland. In 1770, in his first year at the Royal Academy, he carried off a silver medal, following it with a gold medal in the following year. He was a first-class artist and engraver who haunted the British Museum in his enthusiasm for the history of our nation, and in his determination to produce his books about it.

His first book, *The Regal and Ecclesiastical Antiquities of England*, was published in 1773. He not only drew the illustrations, copied from ancient manuscripts, of kings and church dignitaries, their symbols of rank, their armour, vestments, seals and other objects of interest, but also engraved the metal plates from which these illustrations were printed. By 1778 he had done a similar work in several volumes on the *Manners, Customs, Arms, Habits, Etc. of the People of England* and a *Chronicle of England*. In 1801 he had published his *Sports and Pastimes of the People of England*, which has been republished in the last twenty years. All of his illustrations have been used time and again by later authors of books on these subjects, striking testimony of Strutt's ability as an artist, engraver and original researcher.

Inevitably Joseph Strutt had little connection with Springfield Mill once he had started on his artistic career, but it is a pleasant thought that he may have returned from time to time to the old family home to stand on the bridge and watch the millrace churning in its course to join the Chelmer. The last miller here was Alfred Bradridge. It was he who discarded the great water-wheel in favour of a turbine, a screw-shaped propeller turning under the water, able to cope with shallow conditions which defeated the big wheel. Yet like so many mills on the two rivers, Springfield was made redundant by great changes in trading resulting from centralized manufacture. By 1929 it was being rented as a store and workshop, but more recently it found a surprising new lease of life as a restaurant.

Dropping a little further downstream we find that the building of a new bridge over the Chelmer in Springfield Road in 1819, when it was actually part of the parish of Springfield, was thought by John Booker in his *Essex and the Industrial Revolution* to have been ". . . the worst blunder of its kind in Essex in the nineteenth century." Thomas Hopper was the County Surveyor at the time. He reported on the existing bridge, which was still made entirely of timber in the tradition and style of the medieval bridge builder. With the Industrial Revolution dawning, Hopper suggested and designed an iron bridge on brick supports. One of the contractors who tendered for construction, eager for the prestige of working with the County Surveyor, was Ralph Dodd. Hopper recommended him to the Trust responsible then for the bridge, even though Dodd passed over Hopper's own plan and advocated a suspension bridge. Dodd hoped that innovation would lead to more business in iron bridges throughout the county, with his firm supplying them.

It went wrong from the outset. Material earmarked to be reused was found to be rotten. Then, through a bad mistake in calculation, the Trust was put to the expense of buying up part of the garden of a house next to the bridge to provide an adequate approach. As soon as it was completed doubts were expressed about its safety. For seven years it just about held together, to the end of the period of the bond demanded from the erectors for rebuilding at their own cost if it did fail. John Richmond, the Chelmsford engineer whose tender had been rejected, was then called in to make major repairs before the bridge could be passed as serviceable. By that time the cost had risen to nearly twice the sum originally estimated. As Booker said: "Altogether it was a dismal business." The present bridge was built with less fuss and more efficiency in 1913.

The Chelmer does not pass under the main street of the town; it is the Can which is crossed by the Stone Bridge at the bottom of the High Street, but since the Can joins the Chelmer here in the parish of Chelmsford we can regard this bridge and the other at Springfield Road as one of the chief causes of

The stone bridge over the Can at Chelmsford. *Fred Spalding.*

Chelmsford's growth as the county town. The Romans had bridged the two rivers to bring their straight roads from London through Moulsham and on to Colchester via Springfield. The Saxons did not have the bridge-builder's art to mend the derelict Roman timberwork. They found the shallowest places and forded the rivers. One ford was on or near Coelmer's land; so that settlement was known as Coelmersford. As the name changed with the ages so Chelmersford developed, and people naturally concluded that this was the ford of the Chelmer. The name stuck and the river was christened.

The Stone Bridge was first built very soon after Henry I ascended the throne in 1100, to the order of the Bishop of London, Maurice, who was Lord of the Manor of Chelmsford at that time. He had the foresight to see that with the two rivers bridged his manor could be improved with the tolls and trade of a busy market centre. Subsequent Bishops built on his vision, and in 1199 Bishop William was granted the right to hold a weekly market on Fridays. That led to increased use of the bridge and many an argument as to who should repair it, since one half was judged to be in Moulsham, which was owned by the Abbot of Westminster, Lord of the Manor there. By 1351 it was on the verge of collapse, especially on the Moulsham side. The Abbot reluctantly made first-aid repairs, and ten years later the timbers of the deck of the bridge were replaced.

So the old bridge was made to last through another ten years. Then the Bishop and Abbot agreed that it must be rebuilt. The Abbot commissioned the top specialist to design a new bridge. He was Henry Yvele, master mason to King Edward III. When it was finished in 1372, made all of stone, it had three arches and earned the title of the Stone Bridge. So well made was it that it took all the constantly increasing traffic for the next four hundred years. Its importance is recognized by its inclusion in the coat of arms of the Borough of Chelmsford.

It was rebuilt under the supervision of John Johnson, surveyor to the county, by 1787. He designed the single span bridge we see today, with the date shown on the keystone. In taking the abutments out into the river the flow at flood times was much obstructed and added to the severe flooding experienced on many occasions at this end of the town right up to 1962, when a very successful flood relief scheme, including the concreting of the river's banks on its way through the town centre, was undertaken by the Essex Rivers Board. The bridge will not be altered again, for it is scheduled as an ancient monument and its preservation is ensured. Interested observers will note that the balusters of this bridge are not made of stone at all but of that clever imitation, Coadestone.

We cannot leave the county town without reference to its principal modern architectural feature. The thrusting, thriving new Chelmsford is characterized by the grand extension to County Hall in the centre of the town. It was opened by Her Majesty the Queen on Friday 29th July, 1988. She marked two milestones in the history of Essex when she said:

Even for a county with as rich a cricketing tradition as Essex the century is still cause for celebration. This year Chelmsford is celebrating the centenary of the granting of its Borough Charter and next year the County Council, at present ninety-nine not out, will enjoy its own centenary; jointly you will have achieved that rare feat, a double century partnership.

What a happy coincidence that the completion of this elegant new extension to County Hall should fall at such a time. I share your confidence, Mr Chairman, that the building's many virtues will go towards still higher standards of service to the Essex community and I add my congratulations to those whose foresight, skill and hard work have inspired and completed it . . .

The extension to County Hall being officially opened by Her Majesty the Queen, July 1988.

Up to the main entrance, steps and ramp rise in plum-red brick. Just inside the doors of the fifty-eight foot high atrium two glass columns rise up, naming every town and village, with engraving which recalls the county's maritime tradition and its abundance of windmills. This glass sculpture is by Alexander Beleschenco, who has used thousands of pieces of coloured glass to transmute light in interesting variety. All the upper floors are visible, with lifts rising and falling like shuttles of glass weaving some great tapestry. Further into the atrium, beyond the reception desk, fish swim and fountains leap in a water feature which would not disgrace the Chelsea Flower Show. Down a flight of steps, in the semi-basement, beyond a large exhibition hall, is the Chelmsford library, directly opposite the new Register Office. The office nearest the entrance is sensibly the Tourist Information Department, packed with leaflets freely available on all aspects of life and leisure in the county.

Whilst we move on via the race-track of the ring road and its roundabouts to Moulsham Mill the river slides past the unsightly dereliction of the old gas-works and the carpark, called nostalgically King's Head Meadow, to its confluence with the Can. Just before they meet the Can is crossed by a Bailey bridge, the type used by advance forces in the Second World War, which was carried by a tracked vehicle and winched across a river at a moment's notice. The strength of such a bridge can be judged from its use here for twenty-five years.

Until 1962 the Chelmer, strengthened by the Can, passed under Moulsham Mill. The flood relief scheme dictated that the course of the river should be straightened, and only a depression in the earth indicates the former route. This did not affect the mill, for that had been supplemented with steam-power since around 1840 from a brick-built mill behind the present white, weatherboarded water-mill, which was built about 1780. The steam mill was yet another one of several installed by those enterprising twins, William and Henry Marriage.

There has been a mill on this site from the beginnings of recorded history. Owned from Saxon times by "The Abbot and Monastery of St Peter's, Westminster", it was being leased in 1534 to John Longe. When Henry VIII took over their property from 1531 onwards, Thomas Mildmay bought it and rented out the mill just as the monks had done. From 1667 the Strutt family ran it. They rebuilt it during their tenure, as shown by an inscription on a beam discovered during Marriages' renovations in 1891 which reads: "John Strutt, miller, millwright, built this mill, Bishop's Hall, 1716." The mention of Bishop's Hall obviously refers to the fact that at that time the Strutts were not only running that mill but using it as their headquarters.

The Bullens followed the Strutts as millers at Moulsham. Business was good enough when Abraham Bullen died for the Beeleigh miller, John Crosier, to confide to his diary: "A man who by the prosperity of his trade, his own industry and living very closely, amass'd a good deal of wealth." A younger Abraham Bullen was still leasing the mill in 1813, when he was allowed to demolish the windmill which had stood close at hand for centuries.

When the Mildmays sold the mill in 1917 it was described thus: "Moulsham Mill is built partly in Brick and partly in Timber, with a tiled roof on four floors and is fitted with an Undershot Water Wheel; the whole of the Trade Machinery being the property of the Lessees. It has been one of the best-known Corn Mills in the District for many years." The sale catalogue should have added that it was converted to roller milling in 1891, though the old water-driven stones were retained. In the same year as the sale electricity was introduced to drive a pair of stones grinding wholemeal flour. Though it was constantly being modernized to keep up with latest means of power the water-wheel was still used to provide stone-ground flour up to 1958, and was one of the very last water-wheels in the county to turn productively.

In the era before the railway the importance of Moulsham Mill was undeniable. A wharf was constructed right beside it so that wheat and coal could be brought up the canal from Maldon and unloaded with ease. Millers were enterprising men; they knew the farmers who brought corn to the mill would go back with empty wagons, and they were just the wagons to transport the coal which was the vital fuel not only for the farmer's house but also for the steam-driven machinery then being introduced into agriculture. The miller needed coal as well to drive his own newfangled steam-engine, which at last ended his dependence upon the unpredictable flow of the river.

The Chelmer was transformed into a canal just below the mill and before the bridge which takes the Chelmer Road across it, built in 1932 as part of what was then the Chelmsford bypass. So begins a new chapter in its story.

CHAPTER THREE

The Blackwater from Source to Panfield

WHERE does the Blackwater start? There is still some doubt. People in Debden claim that it starts there on the perimeter of the old airfield, but folk around Sewards End like to think that it rises in the field north-west of Tiptofts, an old manor house. All of them are quick to point out that it is in any case the Pant, which like a pop-star assumes another name later in life as it reaches maturity down at Bocking.

Pant was originally the name for the entire length of the river, from source to sea. It is only since about 1848 when White's map was produced that the section downstream from Kings' Bridge at Bocking has been called the Blackwater. P. H. Reaney, the place-name expert, traces Blackwater back to a mention of "le Black Water" in a Manor court-roll of 1477, but he also says that the Pant gets a mention in Bede's *Historia Ecclesiastica*, which was written in the eighth century. This is reinforced by the use of this name for the river in the famous poem, the Battle of Maldon, composed very soon after that battle in 991. Since *pant* is Welsh for a valley, and the Celtic tribe which first settled in the forest of Essex probably had that tongue, it would seem that this is the historical name of the river. Perhaps it was Norden, the map-maker, who started the confusion back in 1594 when his map of Essex showed the whole length of the river as the Blackwater; he referred to the "Pante" in his description as only a "smalle river".

In the Tiptofts direction the first evidence of the birth of the river is a line of greener, damper vegetation in the fold of a field. By the time it arrives at and goes under the drive to Tiptofts it has grown into the tiniest stream, though a couple of dry days in summer are enough to make it sink shyly down into a tangle of vegetation. At Tiptofts itself Mr Ian Haigh showed us how a natural spring from the gravel bed of the moat overflowed at one corner to add a widow's cruse of a trickle to the tiny stream. That spring was the household's only water supply until the 1930s. The house, with an Edwardian facade of about 1910, stands within this well-preserved moat, a feature not unusual in this

Left: The source of the Pant from the drive to Tiptofts.

Tiptofts viewed through the trees across the moat.

part of the county, for at least seventeen moated homestead sites have been identified here in Wimbish. Fred Roe explained in 1929 why Tiptofts was so remarkable:

> Dotted about all over the map of Essex are numerous houses of pre-Reformation times which have once possessed open dining halls; now partitioned into compartments by timberwork and panelling of Elizabeth's expansive reign. The most wonderful of all these ancient residences is Tiptofts Manor House, near Wimbish . . . here we have a very good survival of the internal arrangement of a substantial landowner's residence some twenty years before the Battle of Crecy [1346] had been fought and won.

We were stunned with excitement and pleasure at seeing the lofty interior of the hall as it was nearly eight hundred years ago, and our feelings were intensified as we slipped out of the brilliant sunshine which bathed the modern exterior into the muted light of the past. From a mellow, flagstoned floor the timbers soared upwards to the rafters of the roof, which was supported by a pillar fashioned from an oak tree in the very likeness of a stone column, a feature to be found in the churches of the thirteenth century. The nearest comparison might be the row of timber pillars forming the north arcade in Shenfield church, though these are two hundred years younger. A second column of this pillared hall can be seen incorporated in a later wall, and further evidence shows that the hall in its original state had two aisles. Here the local lord sat in medieval splendour and was served by his vassals from the buttery, kitchen and pantry, each having its own arched entrance.

The unusual name of the house, Tiptofts, is derived from the family of Tippetoft of whom John is shown as the owner in a record of 1346. In former times it was known as Wantons because John de Wanton, who was Sheriff of Essex and Hertfordshire in 1331, had become lord of this manor some time before his death in 1347. A brass in Wimbish church commemorates Sir John and his wife Ellen. It has been despoiled and the remainder is now covered with a carpet for better protection, but a rubbing of the brass has been put on view at the west end of the church. There is still enough left of it for us to appreciate the charming gesture of the two figures touching hands in love and comradeship.

The manor-house descended through complicated family inheritance to Sir John Mordaunt in 1562, and he left it to Brasenose College, Oxford, for charitable purposes, including the support of three scholars at the college. The

Wimbish church: note the gravestones laid in the shape of a cross.

present tenants, Mr and Mrs Haigh, have furnished the hall with items entirely in keeping with its ancient lineage, including a banner illustrating the arms of the de Wanton family. Tiptofts is now a farmhouse, and the farm has been made to pay its way, but Mr Haig could tell us of the heartbreaking appearance of the place in 1927 when ten prospective tenants came to look it over and all, except his father, turned it down flat because of its parlous condition and the poor outlook for farming in general. His father, one of many Scotsmen whose families took a chance on farming in Essex during the great depression at the beginning of the century, worked tirelessly, ceaselessly, and handed the farm over to his son as a going concern.

There is still one pleasant reminder of the old farming life, standing all by itself in a field. It is a pigeon-house made all of brick under a tiled roof with holes in the gables at each end for the pigeons to come and go at will. It is a handsome building fifteen feet square with about 550 brick nesting holes. When fresh meat was only a memory in the depths of an Elizabethan or Jacobean winter, the pigeons were collected by the dozen to make a grand pie in the kitchen of that aisled hall.

The little trickle from the moat and the natural drainage from the fields sends the young Pant on its way to Wimbish and the junction with its other source stream reaching out from a spot by the perimeter fence of Debden airfield. Vernon Clarke's description, in *Down the Chelmer and up the Blackwater*, of the exact location of this source cannot be bettered: ". . . on the right of the road

The pigeon-house at Tiptofts.

[west from Elder Street] beside the airfield's perimeter fence, at a height of 380 feet above sea level just before the road starts going down towards Debden Cross and the valley of the Cam . . .". The field where the two sources join is on Wimbish Hall Farm, run by Michael Padfield. It has no name, but is simply referred to by the family as the water meadows, and is one of the fields which run down from Rookery Pond, a homely name for a placid lake beneath towering trees, fed by the Pant just prior to its acceptance of the Debden tributary. Upon their union the stream is nothing more than a runnel, deep in its bed, lost in high summer under a mass of grasses, nettles and scrub.

The farmhouse stands on the rise above the stream, along with the church. Both buildings have suffered at the hands of time. The farmhouse, the old Tudor hall, was completely burnt down in 1952. From the ashes arose a house which, with its white timber-cladding, fits well into the surrounding Essex countryside. Mr Padfield runs a mixed farm with arable and some cattle, including a splendid bull in brown and white running with four cows, all black from head to hoofs. We were assured that the bull was most amiable, but we did not test his friendship. The Padfields are all keen riders and they also breed horses. Their pride and joy is the pure-bred Cleveland Bay with the characteristic dark brown body and black legs.

The church of All Saints can only be approached through the farmyard, though the way is so well-metalled and the yard so neat and tidy that this is not immediately apparent. When Miller Christy, the Essex naturalist and historian, came here checking material for his handbook for Essex, which was published in

Wimbish Hall: rebuilt in white timber-cladding.

1887, he said he found ". . .an unsightly west tower of brick built in 1756 and containing 3 bells . . .". He must have been one of the last authors to see it because it was taken down entirely in 1883, leaving the exterior of the west end with a brick scar reminiscent of a chimney stack. Of the three bells two are to be seen on the floor at the west end and the third has been mounted in a frame in the churchyard to continue its ancient function of calling the faithful to prayer. The nave is Norman work, altered in the thirteenth century; the north aisle is fifteenth century. It can be seen that the church has been repaired and restored through the ages by parishioners sincere in their belief. The condition of the church today, beautifully clean and carefully tended, shows that belief continues.

It may not be coincidence that the teasel, with its prickly stem and head of flowers interspersed with hooked bracts, is to be found in this parish, in those ditches and corners where modern machinery cannot penetrate. This was an area where cloth was woven on a very large scale, and merchants like Thomas Paycocke of Coggeshall, who died in 1518, made a fortune from trade in Essex cloth, much of which was exported. The vast flocks of sheep kept in Essex provided the wool, the looms in cottages in the north of the county wove it, and the fullers, as part of their processing work, raised the nap on the cloth by drawing across it the prickly dried head of the teasel, *Dipsacus fullonum*, which was named after them.

A very large number of these teasel heads were required in this operation, so it was a profitable crop for a farmer. Could it be that the teasel we see growing today is a descendant from those days? It has to be said, however, that the untrained eye cannot distinguish between the common, wild teasel and the fullers' variety.

It is here in the scattered village of Wimbish that the united Pant goes under its first road bridge, a very insignificant affair on the narrow lane from Maypole End to Tye Green. Then it turns north east on its course to Radwinter. In this village the Pant appears as a true stream, forming pools in places, then trickling over a gravelly bed beneath the road which runs from the church to Wimbish Green.

The church stands in a commanding position above the river valley. It was virtually rebuilt to the design of Eden Nesfield around 1870, with a tower, crowned with a spire, completed in 1887. There is still beautiful old work to be admired in the arcades of the nave, put up in the fourteenth century, and in the timbered south porch of the same date, with its overhanging priest's room above. These old parts of the church would have echoed on a Sunday to the sermons of William Harrison, a man who achieved national fame with his *Description of England*, published in 1577 as part of Holinshed's *Chronicles*. He was born in 1534 and was Rector of Radwinter for thirty-four years from 1559, with Wimbish parish added in 1571 to give him an increase in his stipend for the next ten years.

Radwinter church from the bridge over the Pant.

His book is a lively account of life in England as it was then compared with what Harrison remembered of his younger days, and an observation on elm trees illustrates the wide-ranging nature of the work:

> Of all the elms that I ever saw, those in the south side of Dovercourt, in Essex, neere Harwich, are the most notable for they grow in [such] crooked manner, that they are almost apt for nothing else but navie timber, great ordinance and beetels: and such hereto is their naturall qualitie, that being used in the said behalfe, they continue longer, and more long than anie the like trees in whatsoever parcell else of this land, without cuphar, shaking or cleaving, as I find.

The "beetels" he mentions are not insects but heavy mallets used in the shipyard for driving wedges and on the land for setting in fence posts. However, in the account of a fight at neighbouring Great Sampford in 1680, John Dench found another use for his beetle. Whilst driving in fence posts he was antagonised by Giles King. He hit him on the head with his stake beetle, killed him, and was hanged at Chelmsford.

Nesfield not only designed the restored church, he also planned the alms-houses, six of them, the village hall, combined with two cottages and a dispensary, a row of cottages and a shop, which replaced the twenty houses

51

destroyed in a terrible fire around 1874. A sign of changing times is the closure of the old Red Lion opposite the church and its conversion to a private house. Back in the nineteen-thirties it was kept by George Garrard who was also a saddler. It could have been Harrison's observations of the things that went on at the inn so near his church which caused him to write:

> I know some aleknights so much addicted thereunto that they will not cease from morrow until even to visit the same . . . till they defile themselves and either fall quite under the board, or else, not daring to stir from their stools, sit pinking [i.e. blinking] with their narrow eyes as half-sleeping till the fume of their adversary be digested, that they may go to it afresh . . .

Whatever would he have said of that day in January, 1642, when the Rector, Richard Drake, a loyal supporter of the established religion, was pulled out of the pulpit and dragged feet first with his head bumping over the floor right out of the church by a local Puritan extremist, called Augustine Hawkins, who had shouted in the church: "Let's have him out of the church and knock out his brains"?

Our next meeting with the Pant must be below Hilltop Farm, on the B1053 from Radwinter to Great Sampford. With only a few grazing sheep for company and the traffic noise muted by distance to a mere hum, we follow a track down to a cattle bridge over the river, which has noticeably grown in size. The wind stirring the ripening wheat and rustling in the trees and the sun shining from a cloud-flecked sky enhance a landscape which is Essex countryside at its best. From here the Pant follows, at a lower level, the contours of the B1053 as it makes its way to Great Sampford, where the river flows under the B1051 just below the church and the junction with the B1053.

Great Sampford from the bridge over the Pant.

Before we follow the river on to Great Sampford let us take a sideways glance at Hempstead, for this is the village which two men, the one famous and the other notorious, could call home. For explanation head for the church. The fame attaches generally to the Harvey family, of whom some fifty members occupy their coffins in the family vault beneath the North Chapel, and particularly to William Harvey (1578–1657), who proved to the world in primitive days of medical practice that the blood in the human body was constantly circulated through the action of the heart. The doctor's memorial in the church is a white marble bust of himself set against a background carved in restrained baroque style. The sculptor, Edward Marshall, is said by contemporaries to have combined a telling likeness with an outstanding work of art. Though we cannot judge the likeness as we stand in the church we can appreciate the rare beauty of the portrait and the skill of the artist. Other monuments put up in succeeding centuries celebrate this same family.

For two hundred years Dr Harvey's remains lay in his coffin of lead, shaped to the contours of his body, with a face actually painted on the lead and an inscription on the breast. Then the Royal College of Physicians felt that his memory should be more obviously honoured. They paid for a sarcophagus made of a single block of Carrara marble to be placed in the North Chapel, to which the worthy doctor's remains were transferred in the course of a rather grand ceremony in October, 1883.

No ceremony marked the burial of Dick Turpin, the notorious highwayman, after he was hanged at York. He was born and baptized in Hempstead, both events being entered in Latin in the church register on 21st September, 1705. His parents kept the Bell Inn and had great hopes for their son, but he disappointed them. He could not keep a job, drifted to the low-life of London, joined a gang of robbers and finally took to the craft of the highwayman, at which he was for a time sucessful. Involved in more than one murder he had to flee from Essex to Yorkshire with a price of £200 on his head. There it was the shooting of a mere cock-pheasant which brought him to jail. He was not recognized as Turpin until he sent a letter to his brother asking for help and money to effect his freedom. His handwriting was recognized, his identity was established, and he never saw freedom again. To those who watched he appeared brave enough as he stepped up under the gibbet on 7th April, 1739.

The Bell Inn has benefited from that family connection; it is even subtitled, as it were, Turpin's Tavern, and shows on its walls prints and copies of old documents concerning the doubtful hero. The bars have been opened up as one large room, with a vast fireplace at one end where huge logs slowly sputter away in winter.

The tourist might well leave Hempstead marvelling at the skill of the old masons who built the tower of St Andrew's. It is not easy to see from a general view that it is really quite new. The former tower fell down in 1882 and the rebuilding was not started until 1933. It stopped the following year when it was two-thirds complete because the final one thousand pounds needed could not be raised. Work started again in 1959, when that final third cost £14,000! It was dedicated by the Bishop of Colchester in 1962.

The story of the Sampford villages, Great and Little, begins in the Old Stone Age with the evidence of a stone axe-head found at Dove House Farm in 1896. Man's settlement here as the years rolled on is confirmed by the Bronze Age snake bracelet also found in the area and now in the Cambridge University Museum. The boulder clay which makes the district so suitable for growing corn has prompted local historian Gerald Curtis to quote the old saw: "The tiller of the heavy Sampford soil must always have expected to eat his bread in the sweat of his face."

Great Sampford was formerly called Old Sampford to distinguish it from the New or Little settlement, though that must have been a long time ago, for they were separately entered in the Domesday-book of 1086. The two of them cover some three miles of the Pant valley from Anser Gallows south-east to Hawkins Hill. According to the Domesday-book Great Sampford had a mill with its wheel turned by the Pant, but Little Sampford's Saxon mill had already ceased operation.

It is interesting to see how many houses and localities still owe their names to early inhabitants. The Lay Subsidy Tax of 1327 required the listing of all people liable to pay it. For Great Sampford it includes Thomas Chakston (Chalkstones in Hempstead), Bartholomew Sparwe (Sparrows Hall) and William de Lacre (Lakehouse Farm) and, for Little Sampford, Simon Maynard (Maynards Farm) and Thomas de Boyton (Boyton End). Free Roberts Farm derived its name from the corruption of Fitz Roberts. A Walter Fitzrobert undertook, in an agreement of 1258, to pay a yearly rent of a pair of white gloves or a penny for this land. Howses is a direct reference to John Howse who was living around 1400.

The south transept of St Michael's, the parish church of Great Sampford, was already a hundred years old in his time. Most of the church dates from 1320 to 1350. One fascinating feature is the long row of stone seats on the north and south walls of the chancel, all arcaded, providing twenty-one seats for the chapter of the rural deanery of Sampford, which included twenty-one parishes. Amongst the carving on the pillars of the south transept going into the south aisle are light-hearted ones of the ploughman and his oxen and of the creatures he would see about him, from the owl down to the humble snail. It is a very complete church of its period, restored in 1938 when the brick stair in the tower was removed. The south door had to be replaced in the sixteenth century. Church Cottages, possibly once the manor house, are contemporary with the church.

It is not known when the bridge over the Pant just below the church was first constructed. It would have been a timber affair requiring constant repair and replacement, as mentioned in the manor court record of 1629. In 1676 the court declared it to be the responsibility of the lord of the manor, then Edward Peck, to effect the repairs which by then were badly needed. Thomas Wright, reporting on the bridge in 1835, made a further point:

> Water is abundant here and of good quality: the rivulet of Freshwell [i.e. the Pant] has a wooden bridge southward from the church, and, in heavy rains and snow-thaws, frequently overflows and causes floods. On these occasions the brook fills rapidly, and covers a considerable portion of the low meadow grounds, rendering the ford impassable. These floods would be considerably diminished by clearing away sand-beds and other obstructing matters, which might be usefully applied to the heavy lands.

West of the church a couple of miles down a lane with right-angle bends is Tindon End, a place which is of some interest to road users because Sir James Macadam made his home in the Manor House, which he renovated and improved, along with the grounds. It was he, Miller Christy said in his *Handbook for Essex* (1887), ". . . introduced the system of 'macadamizing' roads, and who has been styled 'The Colossus of Roads'", but this does not appear to be quite correct. The *Biographical Treasury* of 1866 tells us that John Loudon Macadam, born in 1756, was "known as the introducer of the system of road-making which bears his name . . .". He was sixty when he first applied his scientific training and qualifications to this problem, yet he was so successful that a grateful government made him grants totalling £10,000 and offered him a knighthood. He declined the latter honour on account of his advanced age so it was conferred on his son, Sir James Nicoll Macadam, who, making the most of the reflected glory, was able to cut a dash at Tindon End. His father lived on to the grand old age of eighty, dying in 1836.

Some people say that Tindon is an ancient, slurred, local pronunciation of St John, for the Knights Hospitallers of St John of Jerusalem had their grange here. It was given to them by the daughter and heiress of Geoffrey FitzBaldwin in the reign of Henry III [1216–1272], and the estate is called Friars Farm to this day.

The river bends abruptly from its north-south course and turns eastward in the direction of Wethersfield, leaving the Bardfield villages, upon its southern bank. The great dividing line of modern times between these closely associated villages is the boundary between the local government Districts of Uttlesford and Braintree, as defined in the local government reorganisation of 1974.

Little Bardfield was described as a "pleasant rural parish" a hundred years ago, and the description is no less true today. The church of St Catherine boasts a very unusual Saxon tower, built a thousand years ago, though re-roofed since then and repaired and restored as time demanded. The Hall right by the church is very photogenic, with its gables and its pargeting, but in Victorian times it was described as a good, modern mansion and Nikolaus Pevsner, the expert on things architectural, warns us that ". . . a recent owner has introduced into the house much that did not originally belong. So the antiquarian has to be careful." A pond lies behind it, no doubt the remnants of the moat which surrounded the first house on this site, fed by the brook which passes behind the Hall and church on its way to feed the Pant. The road from Thaxted, which has its own Bardfield End Green, heads quietly east through the village and then follows the brook's course precisely, at a level just high enough above it to keep clear of winter flooding, before joining the road to Great Bardfield, which reflects the meanderings of the Pant in exactly the same way.

Any tour of Great Bardfield should start at Bridge End, for the presence of the river with its life-supporting, ever-flowing water was the paramount reason for settlement in the first place, and that was long before the building of the first bridge. The origin of its name is now lost in the passage of time, though the elements of Old English it contains would indicate that it refers to those first Saxon colonists who made a home here. Bridge End has changed greatly over the last quarter of a century. A directory of pre-war days reveals that the occupants of the old houses which huddled by the bridge made their living as much by town crafts as by labouring in the fields.

Things have changed. Many of those cottages by the bridge, considered unhygienic by modern standards, have been demolished and replaced with houses suitable to the present life of the place. This means greater space and consequently some surprising new views. The demand in Bardfield today is more from tourists than from residents, for antiques rather than for household necessities, but the past is very much in the minds of the present inhabitants, who preserve with pride and pleasure those old houses around the "green" which could be adapted to modern living.

To call it a "green" would seem ridiculous today when it appears only as buildings, including the Friends' Meeting House, enclosed by a triangle of roads. The patch of green made by the Friends' graveyard reminds us that once this was all green, the focal point of the medieval village where the market was held and the maypole set up. The market cross, a substantial affair with a room above it, was pulled down about 1769, a sign of this large village's diminishing importance as a centre of trade. Mysteriously this central green is quite divorced from that other important centre of village life, the church, which stands away to the south-east with only the Hall for company. Usually the Hall and the church in such juxtaposition indicate the site of the original Saxon settlement, so there remains the unanswered question of why the medieval market sprang up at that distance from it. Despite exhaustive research the question cannot be answered, but that hardly detracts from the pleasures to be enjoyed in a stroll round all the places of interest.

The Great Bardfield Cottage Museum was opened in 1961 in a thatched-roofed cottage, which had once been left in a rich man's will to house a less fortunate family. It now houses a varied collection of bygones, including those very items. From the museum one can stroll round that triangle of roads and on to Bridge End, appreciating the village story as shown in its architecture. This includes the public hall, called affectionately the Town Hall, built in 1859 and costing £750. It is now largely concealed behind the four pollarded lime-trees which give a rather gay, French air to the spot.

The river runs away from Great Bardfield, but on its way in earlier days it drove the town mill, the first mill to be driven by the swelling waters of the Pant. Fifty years ago it was being run by Thomas S. Smith of the well-known local family of farmers, but that was at the very end of its life. He had bought it in 1894, along with the windmill, from the Marriage family, to whom he was related. The two mills were linked as far back as 1754 when Jonas Osborne bought the windmill, having leased the water-mill from Guy's Hospital since 1742. Below the mill the Pant spreads in a pool which reflects the white weather-boarding of the timber-built mill, now going grey with age. It is a peaceful spot so far from the road that one can hear the rustle of the wind in the trees which lean over the pool as if admiring themselves in the mirror, the songs of wild birds and the plashing of the waterfall where once the mighty water-wheel revolved majestically.

Great Bardfield Mill on the Pant.

Access to the water-mill is from the lane beside the windmill, now a private house clearly titled "Gibraltar Mill". It is thought that the reason for this name goes all the way back to 1704 when the British seized the Rock from the Spanish and resisted their counter-attack in the following year. It is most likely that the mill was built at this time when patriotic pride was running high. It was very likely that the awful storm of November, 1703, was still fresh in the memory, for this mill was made massively strong of brick, some fifty years earlier than other brick tower mills in the county. It is described in all its structural and technical detail by Kenneth G. Farries in *Essex Windmills, Millers and Millwrights*, so it is only necessary to add that its sails stopped turning around 1930, that it was cleared of most of its machinery and subsequently transformed after two periods of conversion into the modern home it is today.

From windmill to water-mill—and on the footpaths run, up and down the river bank and beside the Finchingfield Brook, which joins the Pant just below the mill, to Finchingfield, that "calendar queen" of Essex villages.

Finding one's way by car from Great Bardfield to Wethersfield via Waltham's Cross is a great introduction to those narrow lanes, sharp bends, little steeps, streams and woods and fields which are the essence of Essex. Names of houses show their antiquity. Hawkins Harvest, for example, incorporates the names of two owners; the Hervys around 1425 and the Hawkyns around 1495. Through a lane wide enough only for a small car, with no passing places, where houses hide in the trees, a bridge across the Pant appears; this is so arranged that in times of flood when it is submerged it can still act as a ford. Just a little upstream a very prosaic modern construction in steel takes pedestrians high above any possible flood level, where the road climbs up to pass by Dunkirk and Petches (John Pecche was involved in a property deal here back in 1270) to the main road, the B1053, where modern Essex takes over with Wethersfield Airfield just a stone's throw away.

What emotions are stirred at the mention of this name. In the middle of the seventeenth century a band of people from this area made the perilous journey to an equally perilous life in the new colonies in America so that they could practise in peace their own religious beliefs. In the last war the Americans came back to Wethersfield and flew the bombers of their 9th Air Force from an airfield specially constructed in record time in 1943–44. The 416th Bomb Group made its first sortie on 3rd March, 1944. By September the Group had moved into France, supporting the invasion, and the Royal Air Force used Wethersfield until July, 1946, when it was no longer needed, but that was not the end of the story. The Americans came back in 1951 and five hundred men and women of

Right: Gibraltar Mill at Great Bardfield, now a private house.

the 819th Civil Engineering Squadron, Heavy Repair, now call Wethersfield home for the duration of their posting.

That has made a considerable difference to life in Wethersfield, but, except for the passage of the odd extra-large automobile which makes the B1053 look like a footpath, there is no evidence of physical change in the village itself. The church of St Mary Magdalen and St Mary the Virgin stands on the brow of a hill in a manner which makes photography very difficult, and the trees which crowd the green below prevent the capture of a general view of the village. Yet what a wonderfully welcoming landmark its thirteenth-century tower must have been for those returning bombers. The body of the church was thoroughly restored in 1876, but it retains so many points of interest in architecture, stained glass and monuments of centuries before the restoration that a visit is a pleasure. It must be said, however, that Wethersfield is a large and scattered parish; beautiful old houses in rural settings can be photographed around the village and its hamlets, like Blackmore End, Rotten End and Beasley Green.

The list of houses of sufficient historical and architectural merit to justify their proper preservation under official supervision is so long that it cannot be reproduced here. Let one entry stand as an example: down the Shalford road, just far enough away from the village centre to allow the brambles to take over at the roadside, stands an ancient farmhouse known as Sims, now divided into

Left: The beautifully restored farmhouse, Sims at Wethersfield.

Opposite: The popular fishing pond at Shalford Hall.

several small and elegant residences restored carefully to show the true beauty of their age. This house was built over the sixteenth and seventeenth centuries, as shown by two specific features. One is the fine, carved bressummer or main beam on the projecting gable of the north wing, which is typically sixteenth century, and the other is the seventeenth-century panel of pargeting which can be seen on the east side. The window immediately above it was the brainchild of an eighteenth-century occupant, and other owners have altered and added to Sims through four hundred years to make it comfortable and convenient to the age in which they lived. Above the conversions and restorations the original chimney stacks still stand, functional, beautiful symbols of Sims' survival. Nobody now remembers who Sims was, but one assumes he was an early owner of the property.

The parish of Wethersfield spreads down to the Pant and there, as a kind of last outpost, we see the sign to Wethersfield Mill, yet another of those tall, white, clapboarded, timber-framed buildings which cause the tourist to gasp and reach for the camera. The setting is idyllic; the mill and mill house, with some of the associated outbuildings, have been converted into the most delightful houses; an enclave in the countryside which includes, tucked away around the back, business offices and a car park. It is all so far away from the main road and from the village centre that it is like another world.

It is difficult to decipher how the river's course has been altered here. It formerly flowed under the mill but was straightened out to flow past it in the interest of taking the extra flow of water injected into the Pant under the Ely Ouse Water Scheme.

The mill is on the very edge of the parish; from its driveway it is but a step across the bridge into Shalford. A rough road opposite the Old Post Office leads down to the church, Shalford Hall and of course the river, which was the very reason for their erection on this spot. Now the church has to be locked, as is common where places of worship are isolated and at risk from thieves and vandals.

The old farm buildings on the other side of the track have been converted into a stunning modern house of unusual design. When we visited it the farmyard, with Dutch barns full of bales of hay, was crowded not only with farm machinery but also with so many cars that it looked like a used car lot. From the churchyard, through the hedgerow and the chestnut paling, we saw the owners of those cars, sitting under huge green umbrellas, all around a large pond, fishing. The pond is very large and held above the level of the Pant by a big embankment. Pond and river are divided only by a well-used footpath taking the rambler downstream as far as Great Codham Hall, which, though miles beyond Shalford, is still in that wide-spreading parish of Wethersfield on the other bank of the river.

Henry Wentworth, a scion of the great Yorkshire family, who died in 1482, lived here, and his son Roger, who received a knighthood in 1487 and died in 1539, was buried in the parish church according to one authority. However, another, Nikolaus Pevsner, says that the altar tomb with recumbent effigies marks the resting place of Henry and his wife rather than their son.

The banks of the Pant can be traced as a green ribbon with the white walls of Codham mill and mill house glinting like a pearl. Driving down to it requires care for the lane is narrow, the hill is steep for Essex, and the mill buildings form an "L" on a right-angled bend. The Ashbys, father and sons, were millers from 1903 until the mill-wheel stopped in 1956. At least once a week the family would have a batter pudding made of flour straight from the mill as the most satisfactory way of testing the quality of their flour. The mill needed its own stream but a second channel was necessary to carry excess water round the mill, under the road and back into the Pant. Crossing the bridge one comes to the B1053 again; it keeps company with the vale of the Pant all the way to Bocking.

The next point of interest, just off that road, is the remarkable construction of the barns at Great Priory Farm, which can be seen by appointment. They were erected in the later days of the small Priory sited some six hundred yards north-north-west of Panfield church. It was attached to the Abbey of St Stephen at Caen shortly after the Conquest and was in lay hands long before the Dissolution when Henry VIII granted it to Sir Giles Capell. Little Priory Farm is down on the

Great Codham Hall and its dovecote at Wethersfield.

other side of the main road. The barns there are also good examples of the local carpenter's art, but the interest today is in the craft centre beside them, called The Six Apples Craft Centre and run by Helen Tabor. It has become a popular stopping place for tourists.

At the bend in the road immediately beyond the Six Apples a signpost points the way to Panfield, a village named directly after the river. The Saxons described their settlement as "open country on the banks of the Pant" and so it has been known ever since. Up to the last war the village had continued in the ways of simple country life. The Directory of Essex for 1937 describes it thus: "Panfield is a pleasant village and parish near the River Pant 3 miles north-by-west from Braintree station . . . the chief crops are wheat, barley and oats and there is some pasture land." The population then was just 286 souls.

Panfield Hall: some parts of this delightful residence date back to 1546.

The heart of this little settlement was, and still is, its parish church, which stands a little to the east of the later development of the village. It is largely of fifteenth-century building, with walls of flint and pebble rubble, with some ironstone. Of course it has had to be much restored. Four hundred years old, the timber-framed south porch shows evidence of this, but it is evidence too of the community's determination that their ancient "community centre" shall continue its functions, and that the faith and the workmanship of preceding generations shall be respected. One former inhabitant is remembered in the most delightful way: a baptismal ewer, an alms dish and a pair of altar vases are inscribed to the memory of Edward Bangs, baptized here on 28th October, 1591. He took the dangerous passage to America in 1632 and his descendant, W. E. Nickerson, of Boston, Massachusetts, came back in recent times and paid for this memorial. The clock in the tower commemorates Queen Victoria's Golden Jubilee in 1897.

Panfield Hall lies to the south of the church. Its oldest parts, on the west side, date from its original building in 1546; the eastern parts were completed in 1583. The initials carved on the mantelpiece in the dining room, "GCF", indicate the owners then as George and Frances Cotton. The mellow Tudor brickwork is a beautiful sight on a sunny day in a peaceful landscape, whilst most of the original hammer-beam roof construction within has survived, and so have some of the windows. Excavations on the south side have shown that this was once a much bigger house on a rectangular plan, enclosing a courtyard and being enclosed in its turn by a moat of which only the south arm and an outer enclosure remain, but what a picturesque feature!

One man who must be mentioned in connection with Panfield is the Reverend John Ouseley, who lived from 1645 to 1708. In 1668 he was appointed Rector of Panfield and stayed there twenty-six years. He was noted for his industry in collecting masses of information on the history of Essex. He did not put it into print himself, but those who did, well-known historians like Newcourt and Morant, paid personal tribute to Ouseley's pioneering work. Yet there is absolutely nothing remaining to tell us of the character or the life of this unassuming man to whom successive historians of Essex owe so much.

From this ancient settlement by the Pant we must return to the B1053 to meet the river again at Kings' Bridge in Bocking.

CHAPTER FOUR

The Blackwater from Bocking to Langford

A T BOCKING cars rush across Kings' Bridge where a great deal of traffic leaves the B1053 to pass through Bocking Church Street on its way to the A131 north of Braintree. The bridge has a footpath on one side only, so very few people risk their lives to read the plaque placed on the centre of the bridge parapet on the upstream side.

This bridge has a very significant place in the story of the Blackwater for it is the exact dividing line between the Pant and the Blackwater as shown on modern maps, though the gazer from the bridge will detect no striking manifestation of this change of name in the quietly flowing stream. Upstream lies the great complex of Courtauld's former factory, the modern development of the site of the Convent Mill, just across the river from the church. The buildings rise so high and broad that the church is quite dwarfed, yet it was a large church for an Essex village in the fifteenth century. It has been altered and repaired as time demanded. For example, the wooden cupola above the battlemented tower was put up in 1887. In times past the church's size and splendour reflected the wealth of the village as a prosperous centre of the cloth trade, and clothiers, grateful for their continuing success, thanked God from their pockets. The special cloth known as "bocking" was still being asked for in the United States until recent times.

The Convent Mill was quoted in records as far back as 1300. In the eighteenth century it was run as a corn mill by the Raven family, but by 1770 it had been converted to process cloth by one Mr Nottidge, a leading local cloth merchant. By 1802 it had switched to corn and back again to cloth. Joseph Savill, a clothier who employed at least a thousand outworkers in Bocking and Braintree, bought the mill in 1812, when the wool trade in Essex was on its last legs. By 1819 Savill had to sell out to Samuel Courtauld and his new silk-weaving enterprise for a thousand pounds less than he paid for it.

Before taking up the story of the Blackwater as it flows from Kings' Bridge let us, in our imagination, walk up Church Street to Bocking Church Street, once a separate hamlet. On the way we shall see a row of solid-looking houses with plaques on their gables which show they were built by the Courtauld company for their workers in 1872. Our goal is the windmill with an intriguing story behind it, standing in what is now a private garden up the narrowest of drives. This white-painted, weather-boarded mill was built around 1721. It passed

Opposite: The weather-boarded Mill by Bradford Bridge, Bocking.

through the hands of a number of millers until 1774 when it was bought by Bartholomew Brown, the miller of Wethersfield. His descendant, John Brown, was landlord of the Bull Inn in this same street around 1840. He was doing a good trade, so when it came to his turn to work the mill he was in a quandary. However, according to local legend, he soon solved the problem; as he could not go to the mill, he decided the mill would have to come to him, and so this very mill was jacked up, hoisted sideways on to a huge cart and carried one hundred and seventy yards, to be set down exactly opposite the inn. John the landlord could become John the miller simply by crossing the street.

The Pant and Blackwater have turned many mill-wheels in the parish of Bocking for a thousand years and more. As we head out of it, bound for Stisted, we see one more of them. It stands by Bradford Bridge in Bradford Street, making a most interesting jumble of buildings. No photographer could do justice to it without a wide-angle lens. The Mill House, right on the pavement, is an old mansard-roofed cottage with a Georgian front added on when the miller, making money, decided to move with the times. It looks lop-sided and jolly, all stucco and pargeting with a strong chimney stack which looks as though it has been added as an afterthought. Behind it rises the white, weather-boarded mill with its lucam, or projecting loading gantry, standing out on its brackets as if straining to get a better view of what is going on in the street. Beside the mill are all the outbuildings, also white and weather-boarded, straggling along by the stream which bypasses the millrace.

We pick up the Blackwater again off the A120 east of Braintree, on the bridge beside Stisted Mill. There has been a mill here from the days of the Domesday Book which recorded that it was then owned by "the Holy Trinity", in other words the cathedral church of Christchurch at Canterbury. From grinding corn for the folk of the village it turned in the eighteenth century to combining that essential function with the running of a pair of fulling stocks, which is a process defined by the *Scientific and Literary Treasury* of 1866 as "cleansing, scouring and pressing cloths, to make them stronger, closer and firmer, which is done by means of a fulling or scouring mill."

The mill-wheel kept the stones turning until about 1945, and up to 1960 it was still connected to the sack hoist to supply a hammer mill then being driven by an oil-engine to produce animal feed. The Metsons, Edward and his sons, were millers here for more than thirty years but they were the last. Now the mill has been converted into a delightful and picturesque home with a wide-spreading lawn open to the road, where an old farm cart, restored, adds a touch of nostalgia.

The original Stisted Hall was built much closer to the parish church, indicating Saxon origin. The Wisemans were lords of the manor in those early days, but by 1685 William Lingwood of Braintree was the owner. It passed eventually to Charles Hervey, who had to change his name to Charles Saville Onley to claim this bequest. It was his son, Onley Saville Onley, who had the old mansion pulled down and the new house built on the present site. As there were no heirs to inherit the Hall it was sold to James Paxman in 1894, when it was reported: "Mr. Paxman, J. P., is now residing at Stisted Hall, a noble mansion of white brick, built about 1825. It stands in a park of 150 acres." When he died in 1922 his obituary said that he "became an engineer and rose by his own efforts and application to a high position in the industrial world. He established the business of Davey, Paxman and Co. in Colchester in 1865 . . . during the war the firm employed 1,500 hands making shells and other material . . . he contributed the Victoria Tower to the Town Hall." The Town Hall was at Colchester and the tower for which he paid is still a landmark of the greatest interest.

From Stisted the Blackwater runs on under Shelborn Bridge to Bradwell-juxta-Coggeshall. That bridge was there as early as 1370 when it was mentioned in the court-rolls as *Schelredebregge*. Bradwell itself was shown on maps until quite recently as Blackwater, while Bradwell was applied to the Hall and the church away to the east. The bridge here at Blackwater over the Blackwater is called, as you might have guessed, Blackwater Bridge. It looks strong and sturdy enough to take the constant stream of traffic along the A120, but that was not always the case. When it was beginning to fail in 1850 Thomas Hopper, the County Surveyor, advertised for tenders for its replacement. He had to consider ideas ranging from a timber bridge made of oak and cast iron bridges costing twice as much to a suspension bridge based on "Dredge's Patent Taper Principle", which at £300 was £50 less than the timber proposal. Hopper approved the suspension

Stisted Hall: a noble mansion built around 1825.

bridge plan even though he had already suffered an unfortunate experience over this design for the Springfield bridge in 1820.

The bridge was built by Charles D. Young and Company of London under the supervision of the civil engineers Dredge and Stephenson and was soon in use, but when the new County Surveyor, Henry Stock, made his first tour of inspection in 1857 what he saw gave him cause for great concern. A detailed investigation confirmed his worst fears: metal girders used were far too thin, cross girders had been strengthened with wooden binders and the whole construction relied for much of its stability on the framing and the piles of the former bridge which had been left *in situ*. Yet another bridge had to be built just as the age of heavy traction-engines was dawning. A giant locomotive like those made by Eddington & Steevenson in Chelmsford could weigh more than ten tons. The Locomotive Act of 1861 limited the weight of such engines on any road to twelve tons. That was far too much for many existing bridges, and special notices prohibiting such heavy traffic were fixed to twenty-three bridges in the county.

The journey from that busy bridge through Bradwell village soon brings one out into pleasant countryside by Bradwell Hall and the church of the Holy Trinity. This ancient parish was called Bradwell, meaning a broad or full-flowing spring, after the stream which rises near the Hall and which in those early days turned an overshot water-mill on its way to the Blackwater.

The old Hall that Thomas Fairhead knew was burned down long since, but the church where his last rites were solemnly observed still stands serenely in the vale of the Blackwater. It has to be kept locked against the mindless vandalism of our age, but on our visit we were most fortunate, for Sunday service had just ended and the Rector stopped to pass a word of welcome and stayed on to show us round the church.

The Blackwater runs on to Coggeshall, where it passes under the Long Bridge. It has been stated that this is the oldest brick-built bridge surviving in England. The sturdiness of its construction is evident, but it must be admitted that it was considerably widened in 1912 to take two lines of traffic. Until then the bigger waggons and the traction-engines negotiated the ford across the wide pool before the bridge. Nowadays that is a pleasant pausing place, where a seat is provided for folk who bring bread to feed the fleet of ducks which appear at the cast of a crumb.

Beside the bridge, on the other side of the road, the Maltings, a new, small development of homes, reminds us that this was once part of the premises of the Little Coggeshall Brewery which stretched from here to the Short Bridge. One old conical kiln roof has been incorporated in the new buildings as an attractive feature. The Short Bridge bestrides the Back Ditch, a very prosaic name for the channel which leaves the Blackwater south-west of the town and runs roughly parallel with the river right round to the Abbey Mill, rejoining the main stream

Church of the Holy Trinity, Bradwell-juxta-Coggeshall.

The Maltings development at Coggeshall.

just south of it and picking up Robin's Brook on the way. Vernon Clarke suggests that the Back Ditch was the original river and the wider stream was made about 1220 by the monks to drive their mill.

Great Coggeshall, the little town, as opposed to Little Coggeshall, the hamlet, is a place of the greatest interest, deservedly a tourist centre. Its latest leaflet lists seventeen places worth seeing. Top of the list is the parish church of St Peter-ad-Vincula on Church Green. It was almost blown down by a land-mine in the last war, but by 1956 it had been rebuilt so exactly as it was before that it gives the impression of being a complete fifteenth-century church in the Perpendicular style. Look for the monument to Mrs Mary Honeywood, now tucked away on the wall of the sacristy.

Other monuments such as the brasses in the floor of the North, or Paycocke, Chapel to John and Thomas Paycocke of 1533 and 1580 point us to the next place of interest, Paycocke's House in West Street beside the Fleece Inn. It was built to the order of John Paycocke around 1500, and despite all the vicissitudes of time it has survived to present to us one of the most beautiful half-timbered façades of the period remaining in the whole country, rich in carved decoration, inside and out. It is now in the care of the National Trust and can be visited. A fine collection of Coggeshall lace, once the staple industry, has been gathered for exhibition within.

The architecture of the town generally is so varied and interesting that it justifies a walk around, and that gives an opportunity to investigate the many antique shops that have congregated here. The Woolpack Inn reflects the importance of the cloth and lace industry in this town from the fifteenth to the seventeenth century, and the relationship of the river with this industry is shown in the sad entry in the church register of burials: "1590. March 17th Nic. Coman slain in the stocks of the fulling mill."

Abbey Farm continues to display that wonderful variety of early ecclesiastical and seventeenth-century secular architecture. It was not photographed because the farmer sensibly pointed out that all the modern machinery about the farmyard would not only hide parts of the old buildings but would also be an incongruous contrast to them. On the other hand it is cheering to know that this is still a farm, taking advantage of all the latest equipment and machinery, just as the monks themselves took advantage of the latest thinking on water-mills when they installed one just after the founding of the Abbey in 1140. The white, weather-boarded mill, crowned with a mellow-tiled, mansard-roof, lies off a branch of the drive to the farm. It was rebuilt in the seventeenth century on the original site. The full technical details of its operation through the years can be found in Hervey Benham's *Some Essex Water Mills*.

One of the warm, human incidents in its long history was the planting of ten lime-trees by Robert Bridge Appleford to celebrate the birth of his ten sons. He was the millwright who had the mill refitted around 1840 to operate as a corn-mill, and then bought it himself in 1879. Yet the Abbey Mill, in appearance, is essentially a cloth-working mill. A long row of conjoined windows up under the tiles gave the maximum light to the weaver at the loom, and the smooth, long façade is not broken by a sack hoist which would have been installed if it had been built as a corn-mill. It did see a change of use around 1820 when John Hall, a well-known cloth manufacturer, had it converted to silk throwing to make ribbon. His reputation locally as a hard employer was such that local people did not allow their girls to take jobs in the mill. He had to bring in thirty-five girls, aged from eleven to sixteen, from such a distance that he had to give them board and lodging in a special hostel.

Following John Appleford, who had harnessed the growing strength of the Blackwater to four sets of stones, was his son Wyatt who ran the mill until 1947, when he was in his eighties. A fair appreciation of this beautiful old factory in the countryside must include Hervey Benham's last paragraph on it: "Because of the beauty of its situation and its structure, the condition and the completeness of its equipment and its ample size, making it easy to inspect, with room for a complete mill museum exhibition . . . Coggeshall Abbey Mill is ideally suited for preservation, and I trust that will be its future . . .".

A few hundred yards downstream man has made the river his slave once again, at Pointwell Mill, on the eastern edge of Coggeshall Hamlet. Down the drive, well away from the traffic, mill and mill house seem lost in a dream. Standing there today it is hard to imagine that this was once the noisiest place in the Hamlet, with the mill creaking under the rhythmic churning of the great water-wheel and the incessant rasping of the grain flowing through the stones. However that was a very long time ago, probably before 1902 when it was put up for sale. In 1933 it was being used as a depot by a milk dealer, Mrs Sarah Pettit, when Kelly's Directory of Essex called it Pantwell Mill. By 1937 the name had been changed in the Directory to Pointwell. It would seem reasonable to associate it with the Pant in this way, but P. H. Reaney, the place-name expert, says that Pointwell derives from the Norman immigrant, Thierri Pointel, who is shown in the Essex section of the Domesday-book as a considerable "Holder of Lands". By 1960, when the old mill was more or less derelict, it was bought and most sympathetically transformed into the house we see today.

From Pointwell the river wanders in a wide meander down to Feeringbury, a large house which can only be approached down its own private drive off the Coggeshall to Feering road. Seen from the shade of the splendid old mulberry trees, the house presents a homely, comfortable aspect, with two gabled wings projecting from the main front where the entrance porch, offset, interrupts the symmetry. Other additions, like the bay window in one wing and the nineteenth-century wings added at the rear, indicate that this has been a family home through some four hundred years, altered for the comfort and convenience of the day. Beautiful lawns and gardens reach down past the lake behind the house.

Pointwell Mill and house; both have undergone sympathetic transformations.

The fact that *bury* is included in its name means that this was the site of the chief manor house of the parish from Saxon times. The estate first belonged to Westminster Abbey, passed to the Bishop of London in 1550, in the person of Nicholas Ridley, and was then confirmed to Bishop Bonner by Queen Mary in 1553, staying in the Church's hands down to recent times and leased to lay tenants. It is plain that Bishop Ridley walked these garden paths, planned alterations and enjoyed the peace of the place far away from London life and responsibilities. It was he who persuaded Kind Edward VI to endow the foundations of the three great hospitals, Christ's, St Bartholomew's and St Thomas's. Maybe his thoughts turned to the peace he had found at Feeringbury as he waited for the sentence of death by burning at the stake to be carried out. He died with Hugh Latimer, another bishop and fellow reformer of the Protestant Church in 1555.

Just below the house, downstream on the same side of the river, stood Feeringbury Mill. Like the Abbey Mill it changed from cloth working to corn grinding, was overtaken by modern methods of manufacture and demolished shortly after the Great War. The road, following the river's course, runs on to the village of Feering, leaving the old nucleus of the village, around the church, on its left. All Saints' church is of fourteenth to sixteenth-century construction but for a change let us have a look at the village inn hard by, the Bell.

73

The Bell Inn at Feering—reputed to be haunted.

When Wentworth Day, late-lamented journalist, visited the Bell in the nineteen-seventies it still had a small shop incorporated, "just big enough for three customers at a time. But enough goods on the shelves to feed three hundred." Norman Woraker, the landlord, claimed that the two eighteenth-century corner cupboards in the bar hide entrances to tiny priest holes, dating back to when the place was a private house.

The Worakers believed that the place is haunted. Heavy footsteps tramp through the Bell even when lights are on and customers are deep in conversation. The ghost has been blamed for various items lost or misplaced down the years, but he is apparently a genial soul who adds to the atmosphere of a building which definitely dates back to the seventeenth century.

From church and inn it is a short distance via the railway bridge to the old main road, now the B1024, which takes us south-west where the other part of Feering grew up to capture business from travellers along the great coaching highway. It is hard to discern where Feering ends and Kelvedon begins for houses, inns and shops continue in an unbroken line of varied architecture all the way down the old Roman road. As is so often the case, the boundary between the two parishes is the river, the natural barrier in the days when the Saxons

74

were settling their territorial limits. The last mill in Feering was where Rye Mill House now stands. The mill bestrode the Blackwater and its stream still runs in its brick-lined watercourse. The most recent record discovered shows it was working in 1908; now it is a fading memory of only the very oldest inhabitants.

On the border of Kelvedon the river turns at a right-angle to run firstly under the bridge at Kelvedon station, then under the main road. Just a few yards downstream the beauty of Easterford Mill can be appreciated. The name derives from the very earliest days of settlement when Kelvedon Bridge had not been dreamed of and this was one of two fords in the parish, the most easterly in fact, and it was touch and go until the seventeenth century whether the parish would be called Easterford or Kelvedon. The mill was also called Rogers' Mill by the locals, after the last miller who operated it as a going concern.

Down the B1024 we find that the old Roman road breaks its line at the south-west end. Could it be that the river was the reason, through some change of course, some catastrophe of flooding in times before record? Here, off the Maldon Road, is the Kelvedon Museum, opened in 1975 through the efforts of the Feering and Kelvedon Preservation Society. The usual exhibits tracing the history of such villages are supplemented with some surprising items, like the loaf of bread baked in Kelvedon in 1916. Further along the road we join the Blackwater again and can look upstream from the bridge at Kelvedon's other mill, Grey's or Docwra's Mill.

Easterford Mill at Kelvedon, as seen from the garden.

From Grey's Mill one can speed along the new A12, the bypass, or take a leisurely ride down the side lane, more coincidental with the course of the river as it runs through its green vale flanked by rich farmland. For a mile or so the wall of Braxted Park, built of hand-laid bricks some five feet high, four and a half miles round, repels the curiosity of passers-by as to what goes on in the big house far away behind its lake.

West of the church the Blackwater runs through an ugly but necessary concrete-channelled weir and under Appleford Bridge. Beyond the bridge is a private drive to Coleman's Farm. It has to be mentioned because there is something here not yet recorded on the latest maps. It is the twenty-four-acre reservoir on the right of the drive, all but two acres of which is covered by water. It was excavated in 1979 and 1980 to provide a winter-fill reservoir holding seventy-five million gallons of water for the seasonal requirements of the 134 acres of Coleman's Farm. The reservoir has been carefully landscaped. A large number of trees of sixteen different types native to the area have been planted and are now of a size which can be appreciated. It is understandable that birdwatchers should be interested in this new habitat. They are fortunate in that the farmers, Simon and Robert Brice, actively encourage the preservation of wildlife on their farm, seen in their membership of the Essex Farming and Wildlife Advisory Group and the Conservation Committee of the Essex Naturalists' Trust. Since the first filling of the reservoir at least a hundred and thirty species of birds have been seen on it.

Simon, in partnership with his father Robert Brice, is the fourth generation of the family farming in the Blackwater valley. The great drought of 1976 and its consequences caused the family to develop the reservoir in a remarkable scheme of self-sufficiency in water. Their mixed crops now have the benefit of powerful rain-guns when real rain has stayed away, and the valuable crop of blackcurrants, grown under contract for a well-known manufacturer of blackcurrant juice, is irrigated and protected from frost in spring by the application of water from the reservoir in a carefully controlled process. At this critical time some two million gallons of water can be drawn from the reservoir in one night to ensure this frost protection. Down by the river itself willow trees are grown to provide the timber for the manufacture of cricket bats.

Colemans, which has been in the family since 1930, is a Grade 2 listed building which was erected about 1488. In its long history it was divided into two cottages for farm labourers, but the Brices have just completed a thorough renovation which has returned it to its former status as a farmhouse, with a smooth greensward reaching down to the bank of the Blackwater. It looks serene in summer sunshine, but when the river turns ugly, in freezing February floods, the house can be surrounded by those muddy waters.

From Colemans it is but a step along the lane to the bridge over the river and a right-hand bend which takes one round to Little Braxted, to meet the

The picturesque Blackwater from Coleman's Farm.

Blackwater again where it runs under the old village mill, last working in 1886. Now the mill and mill house, conjoined in a line across the river, make two separate homes, with their doors giving straight on to the road before it bends abruptly and leads to Little Braxted Hall and the church. Before leaving the mill it should be noted that around 1970 the owner inserted a glass panel into the housing of the machinery so that the wheel shaft and the race below could be seen—a pleasing and unusual reminder of the true function of the building. Long ago the road ran behind the mill to a ford, and an uncomfortable crossing, at the further end of the mill-pool, but when a bridge was built it was thought best to site it in front of the mill.

Little Braxted church.

The Church of St Nicholas is the very paradigm of the English parish church, but in miniature, for its length east to west is just forty-five feet. It was built in Norman times but it shows the loving hand of restoration and renewal through all the architectural periods up to 1884, when the north aisle was added. Right beside it stands the Hall, a perfect partnership in a beautiful setting. Built in Tudor times it has been altered, like the church, to suit the changing ages, but one original, decorative chimney-stack confirms its ancestry.

From here to Blue Mills the bypass, opened in 1964, cuts off Witham from the river. This old market town has changed very much in recent years as it grew to accommodate London overspill population and to provide the immigrants with better housing and opportunities for employment in factories and businesses set up on new industrial estates. This was not the first planned redevelopment of the town. Before the thirteenth century the settlement was centred on Chipping Hill. Chipping, or *cheaping*, was the early English name for a market. Then the land came into the hands of the Knights Templar, who had what might be called a local branch of their order at Cressing. They planned a new town around the bridge over the river Brain, and sold or rented plots on what became known as the New Land, perpetuated in today's Newland Street. The parish church of St Nicholas was not included in the Templars' territory. What we see today is a virtual rebuilding carried out in the fourteenth century, though the south doorway is thought to be some two hundred years older.

Another spate of building followed the discovery of a chalybeate spring about three-quarters of a mile from the town centre. As such waters were reputed to have curative properties, Dr James Taverner wrote "An Essay Upon the Witham Spa" in 1737 to promote the benefits and thereby attract a clientele. He enthused that the spring water "quickens the Circulation, attenuates the Blood, dissolves viscid Humours, opens Obstructions; after which by its austere and styptick Quality, it strengthens the relaxed Fibres, recovers the lost Tone of the Solids, and restores their due Elasticity . . ." and announced that the "success of our Spa having equalled if not exceeded, the utmost hopes that were conceived for it; it is thought proper to acquaint the Publick that constant attendance is given there as usual. The Monthly Assemblies at the Long Room . . . are now put upon subscription, whereby there will be a certainty of meeting good Company. . .".

The ensuing influx of rich patrons spurred the town's inns, shops and businesses to add new frontages in Georgian style to attract their custom, and that period of hopeful speculation can still be detected in the façades along Newland Street today. This interest in Witham as a spa faded away after Taverner's death in 1748, was revived again at the end of the century for a few years then died for good.

The cinema in Witham attracted far more patrons than ever the spa could boast. The Whitehall Cinema was the private house of Mr Bindon Blood, a well-known Witham solicitor, but after the Great War it was turned into a school, Whitehall College. It was bought for future conversion by Witham and Maldon Picture House Ltd shortly after that, but it was not until 1927 that a William Gaze acquired it and turned it into a cinema, which was opened with great publicity and showy splendour in December, 1928.

From the flickering images on the silver screen we return to the rippling reflections on the river where the Blue Mills were once so busy. Blue Mills is really only one mill. The name arose because it had two mill-wheels in the stream—an unusual sight. "Blue" is, for some experts, an indication of an earlier fashion to paint the woodwork blue, and there is much support for this in that barn doors, wagons and other woodwork about farms in Essex were painted blue. Some farmers swore it kept the flies away. Another school of thought suggests that of the three mills in Witham this was the lowest on the river, that is "below" the others and hence "blue".

The mill finished work early in 1895, though the man who bought it then had the ingenuity to run a dynamo off the wheel to light his Georgian-fronted mill house, separated from the mill itself by an adjoining cottage. Now the mill can be seen as an elegant, white weather-boarded house, with the sack hoist loft still retained, running the height of the mansard-roof. The striking clock on the gable is not a modern feature. It was placed there more than a hundred years ago.

The next stop on the river is, or was, Wickham Mills, another mill given a plural name because it ran two huge wheels, one of them twenty-four feet in diameter. At the height of its power, around 1880, it was working fourteen pairs of stones, with a steam-engine installed to keep up regular production when the river level fell. Sadly this mill, with two hundred and fifty years of history and service to the community, was demolished in 1975 without the least interest being shown in its preservation by those responsible for the environment and its heritage. An application to convert it into a house was turned down, after which the mill fell into that state of dereliction where it could be demolished as "dangerous".

Wickham Place, with its beautiful Georgian façade hiding the original mill house, survives in a setting of peace which would have been unbelievable when the mill shook to the noise and vibration of the water-wheels and those fourteen sets of mill stones.

Another place of peace in which to enjoy the atmosphere of Wickham Bishops, as it was when Philip Morant, the original Essex historian, was rector here for three years from 1742, is found by crossing the bridge, climbing the hill and following the B1018 round the sharp bend to a rough track on the right leading down to that old, ruined church of St Bartholomew, where Morant's voice echoed round throughout those long sermons on a Sunday morning. To the architectural expert the "only remaining feature of special interest is the southeast quoin of Roman bricks, evidence of the Early Norman origin of the church", but such a dismissive view does not allow for all the folk who crowded in here through more than eight hundred years, greeted friends and fellow men, prayed hopefully, praised lustily and were buried reverently.

The present church, which everybody knows because its spire at the top of the hill is such a landmark, stands to the north-east, much closer to the modern

The old church at Wickham Bishops.

residential area in this spreading parish. It was built in 1850, funded solely by a Miss Leigh, to a design of Ewan Christian which is so traditional that it looks much older than it is.

The river hastens away from Wickham Bishops, flowing through fertile farmland to Langford Bridge, where the Saxons made their crossing by wading waist-deep in the water. It was a risky undertaking as the river was wide here; they called it the Long Ford with some feeling, and the name stuck, though slightly changed. Now we can stand on a well made bridge and read the plaque which records its rebuilding in 1924 by Essex County Council.

Two apparent rivals for the Blackwater's favours face each other across the road just past the bridge. One is Langford Mill, the other is the Langford Water Works. In fact they never have been rivals, because the mill had ceased operation by 1918, before it was bought by the Essex Water Company so that its race could be used in the general scheme of treatment and distribution of water for domestic and commercial consumption.

To take the journey through Langford in chronological order requires a step further down the road to the church of St Giles. It looks a strange amalgam of stone, stucco, timber and tile after its thorough restoration in 1882 under the supervision of architect Edward Browning. The strangest feature is the oldest—an apse at its western end. It gives the church an unusual appearance, its roof shaped like an upturned boat, with the pretty wooden porch, its clock and its bell seemingly added as an afterthought. The doorway within that porch, along with the apse itself, are the only surviving evidence of the church's Norman origin.

Langford Mill stands up bold and square, even in its obsolescence, looking for all the world as if it has been made from a set of Lott's bricks with panels of yellow bricks outlined with red strips. The sack hoist loft, in white weather-boarding, stands out prominently from the centre of the roof. The hum of the waterworks extraction machinery gives one the illusion that the mill is still busy at work. In fact the stones had been driven by a steam-engine from some time before 1870, supplementing the water-wheel when the river level fell. The mill we see now is a rebuilding of 1880 after the previous mill was destroyed in a disastrous fire in March of the previous year.

The man who literally left his mark at Langford was the miller Nicholas Westcombe. He had a survey made in 1792 for the purpose of making the Blackwater navigable from his mill down to the junction with the Chelmer and the tide below Beeleigh. As a result a channel was dug out by July 1793. When the Navigation Company took over at that time, they dug across the Langford Cut, as it was called, and took their canal on to Heybridge. The lower half of Westcombe's "Cut" was allowed to silt up where it carried on through what is now the Maldon golf course.

CHAPTER FIVE

The Canal

THE GREAT happening which linked the Chelmer and the Blackwater for ever in the minds of Essex people was the construction of a canal called the Chelmer and Blackwater Navigation, which used the waterways of both rivers to link Chelmsford with the coastal trading ships that unloaded at Maldon. Chelmsford merchants who supplied a thriving market in the county town saw early in the eighteenth century that the cost of transport could be cut by such a direct link, which would obviate also the risks and the delay of slow-moving wagons negotiating the muddy Essex lanes. The off-loading of large cargoes into the capacious holds of barges for forward shipment directly to a wharf in the Springfield area of Chelmsford was very attractive. Money could be saved by bulk transport, and storehouses set up on the wharves could guarantee a constant supply of goods to the local shops and markets.

Since the Saxons themselves had seen the value of the river in so many aspects of their life in this new land, it is not surprising to learn that men of a more modern age had sought to introduce a scheme for a canal, using the Chelmer, as early as 1677. Andrew Yarranton was the chief protagonist; he put the cost of the whole project at £8,000. In the money of the day this was a huge sum. Much of it would have been laid out in compensation to landowners and to millers for the damage and disruption which would inevitably be caused through the establishment of varying levels of water after the installation of locks. The cost was more than the local merchants and investors could contemplate, so nothing came of it.

In 1733 a surveyor from Newbury, J. Hoare, made another proposal that the Chelmer could be utilized for this purpose, once locks had been strategically sited. His estimate of £9,355 was still too large a barrier for the interested parties to take in their stride. At this time too there was a noticeable growth of opposition from Maldon merchants, who saw clearly that they would lose a considerable volume of business if barges took cargoes directly up the river from ships in the estuary.

Left: Barnes Mill as it stands astride the river.

The idea persisted however and was encouraged by no less a person than Sir William Mildmay, who numbered amongst his extensive properties in England the Lordship of the Manor of Chelmsford. Under his aegis a much more determined band of local men met and talked, and their deliberations resulted in a scheme being drawn up by the engineer, Thomas Yeoman, whose plan survives. This time the opponents of the scheme, landowners all down the river and the merchants of Maldon, under John Strutt of the well-known milling family, were actually won round to a rather grudging co-operation. Once again, though, the cost gave backers cold feet; of the £13,000 needed, guarantees totalling only £9,000 could be canvassed.

Yet another scheme, suggested by Peter Muilman in 1772, failed to get off the ground, but by the last decade of the century bulk supplies of many different goods and materials, like coal, timber, lime and manure, were so much in demand by an expanding population all around the county town that it was obvious that less handling and more direct delivery could cheapen prices and increase orders.

The Borough of Maldon was adamant, however, in its opposition, so the Act of Parliament drafted and passed in June 1793 allowed for the canal to bypass Maldon completely and arrive at a junction with the Blackwater estuary at Colliers Reach, off Heybridge.

From the day of opening on 3rd June, 1797, the canal attracted a lot of trade, and continued to do so through forty-five years. In 1842, the last year of that prosperous period, a remarkable total of 60,000 tons of cargo was carried up and down the Chelmer and Blackwater Navigation. The bitter irony was that much of the extra cargo was equipment and other supplies required in the construction of the railway from London to Colchester, which had reached Chelmsford by 1843.

The canal started in what was then the village of Springfield, changing its nature dramatically by bringing heavy industry to its southern corner and tripling its population.

Roughly where Springfield Barnes Farm stands the Chelmer had a fall of about eight feet before it was canalized, so there is no doubt that the earliest settlers saw the possibilities of a mill here. In the fifteenth century this mill was being used for the processing of cloth; a document of 1408 states that Coggeshall Abbey owned the fulling mill here. As Barnes Mill it was one of the Mildmays' properties, described at their great sale in 1917 as "a three-storeyed building substantially erected in brick and timber and slated roof". It still makes an idyllic picture as it stands astride the river, but it has long since been amalgamated with the mill house into one large, well-appointed residence.

At the very edge of the parish of Springfield, now absorbed into the borough of Chelmsford, the lock below Barnes Mill offers a wonderful vantage-point. Here the Chelmer becomes a canal and finally escapes the urbanization of the county town lying below the new, wide-spreading estates, which include the aptly-named Chelmer Village. People have settled into their new houses where thousands of years ago a prehistoric tribe had found the gently sloping vale reaching down to a liberal flow of water and had decided that here was a place where they could live and prosper. Evidence of their bronze-working, their rude huts, their strange religious earthworks or cursus, and their wooden henge, built in much the same manner as Stonehenge, has been found in excavation by Essex County Council in advance of the developers' concealing blanket of concrete.

After the lock at Barnes Mill the canal bends through two distinct arcs on its way to the next lock at Sandford Mill. The two bridges on this stretch are original, specially built just after 1790 as part of the canal works. The horses towing the barges had to change from one bank to the other according to the space available for the towpath. From this point the towpath ran on the left downstream to Little Baddow, then on the right bank to Hoe Mill, four miles on, then on the left bank for two miles to Beeleigh, from there on the right bank to Chapman Bridge and finally on the left bank all the way to Heybridge Basin. Each time a change was made a new bridge had to be built across the canal.

Passing through the Cuton and Stoneham's Locks the bargee of old followed the sharp right-hand bend the river made at the back of Boreham House to arrive at King's Lock, or Little Baddow Mill Lock, where today the point of interest is the wide-spreading mill pool in front of two waterfalls with the deep lock on the other side. The Little Baddow mill had been rebuilt less

Looking upstream of the canal from Little Baddow Lock.

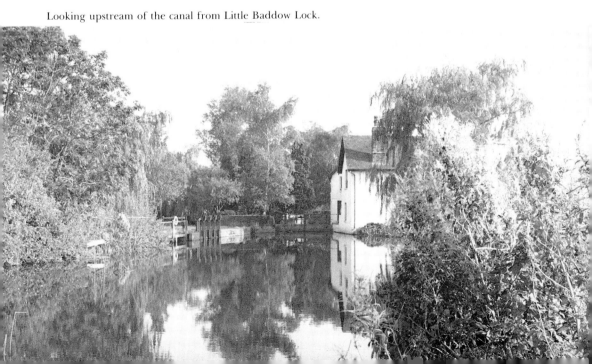

than twenty years before the canal was opened in 1795. It could take advantage of the new transport by water to distribute its ever-increasing output of flour. Steam was introduced quite late, around 1860, when John Piggot ran this mill in tandem with his Langford mill. From his wharf at the Springfield end of the canal he could send his flour on by the very railway which was by then starving the canal of cargoes.

But the decline of local milling was setting in and in 1880 Piggot had to sell Little Baddow mill for less than he paid for it in 1824. Edward Morgan was the owner in 1892 when one June night he had worked late to take advantage of a good head of water. Half an hour after work stopped somebody noticed smoke. It took nearly three hours to gallop off for help, call out the horse-drawn fire-engine and steer it down to the canal bank. By then mill and mill house were just a smouldering ruin.

The Navigation Company built a house on the site, from which a coal business was carried on, using the bulk-carrying capacity of the canal barges. Owners George Smith, until 1899, William King, until 1914, and subsequent tenants used part of the house as a tea-room up to the nineteen-sixties, much appreciated by walkers, cyclists and, above all, fishermen.

Below the house Boreham Brook brings its tribute to the Chelmer and Boreham Bridge affords a pleasant view in both directions, with anglers of all ages very much in evidence. A few paces downstream, where Sandon Brook helps to swell the Chelmer, there is a clear view of Little Baddow church, dedicated to St Mary the Virgin.

The confluence of the canal and Sandon Brook below Boreham Bridge.

Higher up the road, at a junction, stands another church, the Independent Church founded in 1708 by a nonconforming minister from Chelmsford, who, under the Five Miles Act then in force, could not practise his religion within five miles of any town or of his last ministry. Great men like Thomas Hooker and John Eliot, driven eventually to the New World to escape persecution for their beliefs, preached here at Little Baddow to large congregations of people who specially journeyed out of town to hear them.

From the parish church a footpath, little used now, runs direct to the riverbank and the bridge called Black Bridge by older natives but known as Boreham Bridge to the fishermen who make this place their Mecca. Right by the bridge, upstream, enters the flow of a humble rivulet which has its origins well north of the A12, on the far side of the parish by the former Boreham airfield, now a rally centre for the Ford Motor Company. Hardly worth mentioning in association with the Chelmer or, more properly, the canal, you might say; yet when Coates, under Rennie, diverted this brook into the new canal it could supply in volume a total of thirty locks-full of water each day. At the height of the canal's importance that made a great difference to the waiting time for barges as they progressed up or down the long ladder of locks to Heybridge and back.

That supply is reduced to a trickle today, but once it was strong enough to turn a mill-wheel. The dereliction and demolition of Boreham Mill has gone almost unnoticed, but not unrecorded. The Parish of Boreham was most fortunate when the Reverend William J. T. Smith took the living, for here was a man with the greatest interest in local history, and with the ability to write about his detailed historical research in such a way that it could be readily understood by people who were not experts themselves but who did like to know the story of the place in which they were putting down their roots.

The Reverend W. J. T. Smith's *Boreham Histories* includes "Mill and Millers". This is the most complete account to be found anywhere. He traces the erection of a mill on this brook to 1086 at least, for it is mentioned in the Domesday-book. The last mill, which existed until its demolition in 1936, was sited on the right-hand side of the main road going towards Hatfield Peverel, before Boreham House. It was a building of sixteenth or seventeenth-century construction. The discovery of a Tudor brick arch and the massive timbers which framed mill and mill house give credence to the earlier period.

There were two reasons for the eventual demolition of the mill. One was the widening of the A12, then the main road to Colchester, which shouldered it aside. The other was a series of events set in train by Henry Ford's purchase of Boreham House around 1930, together with part of the estate. Tenants of farms were given notice to quit and so business for the mill fell away. The Thrifts left in 1934 and by 1936 all that history was but a heap of timber under a cloud of dust. Interestingly a newspaper of the time reported that "the old oak timbers from both the mill and the mill house are being carefully taken down, and are to be re-erected at Little Waltham." Irritatingly it did not say where in Little Waltham these last relics of the Boreham mill might still be seen.

The church of St Andrew at which Richard Thrift, who died in 1915, was said to be an "improving organist", owes its foundation to the Saxons. Remains of that Saxon church can still be seen in the quoins of Roman bricks forming the east end of the nave and more dramatically in the great chancel arch for which the Saxons again used material they had found in some local Roman ruin. The Normans enlarged the church—witness their sturdy tower. The nave was built in the early thirteenth century. Later in that century a chapel was built in the south aisle and the craftsman who carved its now mutilated piscina was probably the man who made the unusual six-sided font. The Sussex chapel dates from the sixteenth century, and a later addition is the vault under a "porch-like structure" on the north side of the chancel to contain the coffins of members of the Tyrell family.

What is the most poignant reminder of days gone by in Boreham? You must turn to the registers for that. They still exist for all the years from 1559. In eighteen volumes they tell the story of the people of the place—the families that faded, the names that survived, and, amongst them all, the entry in the burials in 1593: "H. Mother Haven suffered at Borham for Witchcraft." The "H" beside the entry could mean that the poor woman was hanged after trial at the court in Chelmsford, but it is more likely to be the clerk's Latin shorthand for *Humo* implying that her body was roughly cast into a hole dug in the ground outside the churchyard, without a burial service. How repulsive to think that people of those days could hunt down poor old women and brand them as witches. In Mother Haven's case there was a strange sequel. When work was put in hand on Boreham aerodrome (it was opened on 6th March, 1944) it was said that a human burial was disturbed by the giant bulldozer, for human bones came to the surface. Villagers said it was the witch's grave, and one or two of the more superstitious amongst them declared that a disease afflicting their cattle at the time was the witch's revenge for the desecration of her grave.

Having been all round the parish, let us home in on the centre of the village, turning down the lane by the Red Lion to return to the church and to the chance of refreshment at the Queen's Head. On either side of the lane spread the estates which have brought what older village folk might justifiably call a population explosion. They well remember the days, not so very long ago, when all was fields and trees, except for a group of sixteenth-century houses, now lovingly restored, grouped together with the church, the pub and the school. In their time the watercress still grew in beds down by the river, where pleasant walks could be enjoyed.

Percy Shelley ran the Queen's Head from August, 1939, through six difficult years of war and on to the nineteen-seventies when at the age of seventy he handed over to his daughter Margaret and her husband Roger Smith. Percy befriended the Americans building the airfield who must have felt so far from home, but that airfield brought bombs to Boreham. Many houses were damaged by blast but the Queen's Head, essentially a sixteenth-century, timber-framed construction, simply leaned with the blast, then settled back again, the only casualty being a window sucked out in the wake of the explosion.

The Cock Inn stands up on the main road. Though it has been modernized within to make one large bar, the old beams which formed the bearing for the internal plaster walls have been left in place and they show clearly the age of this hostelry which catered for the traffic on the London to Colchester road from Elizabethan days. Just down the road beside it stood the medieval manor-house of the Porters. This was totally demolished in September, 1969, as the bypass cut clean across it. By a stroke of good fortune an archaeologist noticed the neglected house awaiting its fate, and made a complete survey of it. His typewritten report on this fourteenth-century, timber-framed house is available in the Chelmsford Library.

The Cock, the Red Lion and the Six Bells have moved into the twentieth century with bright lights, canned music, one-armed bandits and "food at the Bar". The church tower overlooks it all with that solid air of tolerance and stoicism which is the privilege of one with a thousand years' existence.

The river runs on, passing the spot where Sandon Brook joins the Chelmer, to arrive at Paper Mill Lock. It is so called because back in 1792, on what is now an island just below the lock, a pair of mills harnessed the river's energy to grind corn on the one hand and to pulp rags to make paper on the other. This making of paper in the heart of the Essex countryside allowed Little Baddow, on no less an authority than the *Victoria History of the Counties of England*, to claim that it was the first place in Essex where paper was produced. The earliest existing record of a water-mill here was in 1338 when it was part of the Manor of Mowden Hall. It was built to grind corn, then with the introduction of the cloth industry to Essex it was converted to a fulling mill. It is clearly shown on the map drawn up by Thomas Yeoman in 1765 to accompany the proposal for the building of the canal. Very shortly afterwards John Livermore had it altered yet again for the processes of papermaking. At the turn of the twentieth century the premises were being used to make the carbon rods which formed the beam of the first electric searchlights. The old mill's versatile career was ended in 1905 when it was completely burned down.

The Navigation Company set up stables and a bothy at Paper Mill Lock so that bargees and their horses on the way up to Chelmsford could stop for refreshment and a night's rest. That old bothy, which offered only the barest of modern conveniences, was built at the very beginning of this century and has now been restored. The focal point of interest here, despite the view of gushing waters through the weir, must be the last barge to ply upon the canal.

The weir at Paper Mill Lock.

The river-cum-canal runs on in rural retreat. The farm directly south of Rushe's Lock is actually called Retreat Farm. Shortly after the lock, on the left, the little Ter adds her small contribution to the flood. She began her journey twelve miles away near Stebbing Green.

The history of Terling has been lovingly researched and beautifully presented by C. A. Barton back in 1953. His book is now something of a collector's item. The water-mills had disappeared long before then. One of them, believe it or not, had stood in Prittlewell until 1328 when it was dismantled, carried to Terling on wagons and reassembled. In 1868 a tragedy struck the village. Water in the wells was so contaminated after a drought that at least three hundred people caught typhoid fever and forty-four died. A new, untainted supply of water was provided by once again placing a water-wheel in the stream near the Old Dairy Bridge, where the old water-mill had stood. This wheel drove a powerful pump which distributed the uninfected water from the spring in Swan Pond to sixteen stand-pipes erected at handy sites from Church Green to Hare Green. The pumping mechanism, symbol of Terling's triumph over typhoid, went on working until 1916, after which it was carefully preserved by Lord Rayleigh's Farms as an important part of Terling's history.

When the Ter entered Hatfield Peverel it was harnessed once again to the mill which used to stand on the south side of the London road. Since the introduction of the bypass that road must now be called the old London road. It was a big mill, five storeys high, built around 1790 and demolished in 1931, having gone from corn to cloth and back to corn again.

The origins of the ponds to the south of the village are of interest. They were dug out, levelled and banked by the monks and their lay workmen specifically for breeding fish to supply the priory. The spring which feeds the ponds runs on to fall into the Ter.

The foundation of the priory is linked with the name of the village itself. "Hatfield" is of Saxon origin, signifying heathy ground. "Peverel" was tacked on when Ralph Peverel, Norman knight, was rewarded with the lordship of this and other manors. Thomas Wright's history of 1831 tells us how he ". . . married the beautiful Ingelrica, daughter of a noble Saxon, the concubine of William the Conqueror. This lady, in her latter days, repenting her past conduct, to make some atonement, founded a college here in the time of William Rufus, for secular canons, dedicated to St Mary Magdalen, where she spent the remainder of her life, and at her decease, about the year 1100, was buried in the church."

Her son William Peverel converted this "college" into a priory of Benedictines, a branch of St Alban's Abbey, and, though the priory itself was eventually demolished, its church continued as the parish church, replacing the one which once stood up the road to Terling on a little mound above the river. The present church of St Andrew, which overlooks those ponds, consists of the nave of the priory church with a north aisle added in the fifteenth century and a south aisle added in 1873 in the process of a thorough restoration and enlargement.

While the church catered for Christians of the established faith, with outings, meetings, fêtes and all sorts of activities over and above the act of worship, the public houses and ale-houses, seven in all in 1933, offered refreshment, entertainment and relaxation for labouring men after a week's hard work. Let us trace the rise of two of them. The William Boosey—how appropriate!—was given that name only recently. Investigations have revealed that in the time of King Charles I a pair of cottages was being used increasingly as an inn; William Boosey was reported to the court for ". . . enlarging of rooms and increasing a cottage there and receiving of inmates". He was in trouble again in the very next session when he was before the court, as an innholder, because the constables ". . . in their search found John Clarke an idle person in Boosey's house in the time of divine service, and being commanded to depart and repair to church he refused to do so." So here was the inn making a name for itself—and something of a reputation!

As early as 1639 one of the cottages was being called the Drum. When Boosey made his will in 1650 he left the Drum to his wife Mary, and by 1668 it was thoroughly established as an inn, now called the Crown. A hundred years go by, landlords change, the Crown continues. One family, the Spurgins, held the licence here for forty years until 1807. When landlord Derek Robson showed us round we recognized the kingpost of that original cottage which started it all over three hundred and fifty years ago, but we began to lose track of the extensions and alterations as he showed us inside windows which were once outside and floors on different levels.

On the Green, the oldest part of the settlement, founded long before the main highway brought its own huddle of houses to serve the increasing number of travellers, stands the Cross Keys. It is not the oldest public house in the village, but its landlords can be traced back for more than a hundred and thirty years. It was just a cottage in 1729, sold by butcher John Bayley to William Bunting, the sitting tenant, for £26. In 1841 William Davey was the owner and Joseph Saward the tenant. The most interesting information in the whole story is fifteen faintly pencilled words on the record of sale of 1850: "The cottage within mentioned was burnt down and the beerhouse was built on its site." It was Alfred Lucking who bought the place and built the beer-house. He was a farmer, employing five men and bringing up the same number of children. He died in 1879, but the beer-house stayed in the family until 1903. All through their ownership the Luckings had no problems with their beer supply—the Hatfield Brewery was on the same Green, only four houses away! When Gray and Sons bought it to add to their growing number of beer-houses and pubs, supplied by their brewery in Chelmsford, the sale catalogue said there was "also a timber-and-slated Butcher's Shop" as well as a slaughter house included in the premises—a reminder of butcher Bayley who had set up shop here some two hundred years before.

Hatfield Peverel has a place in English and, in particular, Essex history as the home of several witches. Upon their examination at the Assize in Chelmsford in 1566, Elizabeth Francis, Mother Agnes Waterhouse and her daughter Joan Waterhouse were subjected to questioning by lawyers and judges who believed absolutely that these poverty-stricken, uneducated, country women could have power invested in them by the Devil to wreak all sorts of damage and disease on their neighbours. Mother Waterhouse was hanged. Two pamphlets were printed in that year and from them one can see how naïve the judge, the jury and the people generally were when it came to belief in the supernatural. They could not judge where superstition ended and Christian belief began. The whole story of these "witches" and their miserable fate can be read in books and pamphlets in the Essex Collections in Colchester and Chelmsford libraries.

CHAPTER SIX

The Canal from Ulting to Heybridge

OUR journey down the canal continues, providing a pleasant surprise with the appearance through the trees on the left of the tiny church of the parish of Ulting, a little cut off from the village itself. This is the only church in the course of the Chelmer which stands on the bank of the river, with a churchyard which stretches to the very water's edge. Whilst waiting at the church gate on a sunny Sunday morning we watched a mole digging out a hill of fresh brown soil right beside the gatepost. It worked on, oblivious to the world around, and its lack of fear was a testimony to the peacefulness of this holy spot. The church of All Saints, built more than seven hundred years ago, owes much of its charm to its diminutive size, just forty-five feet long and eighteen feet wide. *Durrant's Handbook for Essex*, published a century ago, tells us it is "a very pure example of the 13th century or Early English style, excepting four inserted windows . . . ". It then rather damps the prospective visitor's enthusiasm by adding that inside "the only object of interest now remaining is a rather plain hexagonal font, probably of the 13th century . . .". It is not so easy to look inside these days because the church has to be kept locked against vandals.

When the course of the canal was being planned Hoe Mill, half a mile downstream, was running profitably and not to be bought out. Consequently the engineers had to dig out a new course for their canal, leading to Hoe Mill Lock, then passing under the road, which meant building a new bridge and joining the Chelmer again a hundred yards or so further downstream. This is a very pleasant place in which to walk about, for here the canal runs in its straight channel some twenty feet higher than the river, which loops round in its steep-sided banks below. Now that moorings have been made available to small boat owners by the Navigation Company, one bank is lined with craft of all sizes and appearance, right up to the deep, gaunt-looking lock just before the bridge, which allows canal and river to meet again on the same level. The sound of water splashing in the lock, the bird-song on all sides, the greenery of the trees and well-watered meadows, the glinting of the sun upon the rippling river and the mirror-like reflections in the slow-moving water of the canal do indeed make this a delightful place. On the one hand can be seen the lock-keeper's house and on the other the headwaters and the tail-race of Hoe Mill can still be detected, though the mill was demolished in 1914 and the house is private.

The importance of this mill can be judged from the fact that 13,259 sacks of

The grounds of Ulting Church gently sloping down to the canal.

The canal and lock-keeper's house at Hoe Mill.

flour were ground here through 1865 and transported away via the canal. Hoe Mill Barns, still marked on Ordnance Survey maps, is the only reminder left of all that commercial activity, when the miller had his own quays upstream and downstream of the mill, with two barges, the *Hopewell* and the *Seven Sisters*, as well as waggon teams to service them.

From the bridge here it is possible to go up through narrow lanes and pleasing countryside to Hatfield Peverel and Witham to the north, to Langford to the east and south to Woodham Walter, where south-east of the church lie the vestigial remains of Woodham Walter Hall. It has a minor but interesting place in our national history, back in Tudor times. It was known until the last century as The Fort. This was the lingering reminder, through oral tradition, of the great house built by the Fitzwalter family in the thirteenth century. A clue to the date may be the royal licence obtained by Robert Fitzwalter in 1285 to take a further hundred acres of land into the park which surrounded his house. Permission to fortify the house with crenellated walls, in the manner of a castle, was also granted, but these were more fashionable decoration than defensive works and earned the place that nickname of "The Fort".

When Thomas Radcliffe, 3rd Earl of Sussex, descendant of the Fitzwalters, succeeded to the estate in 1556 the Hall was showing its age.

In 1573 Queen Elizabeth granted him New Hall, Boreham, in appreciation of his loyal services, and the old house became more and more neglected, to the point where it was finally sold and demolished. Not a stone remains to tell the story. Yet it was here that Queen Elizabeth, as a princess, took shelter from possible assassination in the latter days of the reign of her half-sister Queen Mary I. A strange twist, for back in 1550 it was Mary herself, fearful of attempts on her life, who took refuge here, with a boat at Maldon kept in a perpetual state of readiness to take her to France and safety.

Walk the footpath which skirts the site and you can truly say that you are walking in the footseps of three queens of England, because Elizabeth's mother and Henry VIII's second queen, Anne Boleyn, often visited her great friends, the Fitzwalters, in Woodham Walter when she and they were at the height of their intimacy with the King.

Hoe Mill Lock—and the confluence here of the canal and the Chelmer is a favourite spot for fishing. A quarter of a mile downstream, as the canalized Chelmer runs on in tree-lined solitude, Sugar Baker's Holes is the last lingering reminder of a very important industrial site—a sugar factory, the first in Britain.

The sugar beet (*Beta vulgaris*) was known to the Romans, who ate it themselves and fed it to their animals. A German chemist showed as early as 1747 how pure sugar could be extracted from the beet, but it was not until Britain's blockade of France's source of cane sugar from the West Indies that a determined effort was made, by the French, to exploit the humble sugar beet. By 1816 they had set up two hundred and thirteen factories and were producing some four thousand tons of sugar a year. This amazing breakthrough slowly permeated the English farming community. In 1832 our own Essex firm of farmers, Marriage, Reid and Marriage, set up a sugar mill in Ulting Lane, close by the canal and the easy transport it afforded.

They built cottages beside it for their workers and they changed the farming landscape, with fields of sugar beet waving their spinach-like leaves for miles around. Their optimism and their enterprise were baulked by the comparatively low cost of cane sugar, so the mill soon closed and was eventually demolished. The cottages continued to house farm workers but have now been pulled down.

This was not the end of the story of sugar in Essex, for the industry hung on and slowly developed. In 1935 the British Sugar Corporation was formed, with eighteen factories calling in the farmers' sugar beet, on a strictly organized system of collection, to feed the factories from September through to January. The Second World War made home-produced sugar a vital industry. By 1945 the British Sugar Corporation was producing half a million tons of sugar a year, assuring the weekly ration of sugar to every Briton.

The next point of interest on the canal is the huge pipe which bridges over the canal and the towpath. It carries water collected from the Chelmer and Blackwater Navigation, treated at Langford Waterworks and sent on to the Hanningfield reservoir. It has been estimated that up to thirty-five million gallons of water are taken daily from the canal to satisfy the thirst of the ever-increasing population of south and east Essex. Just under a mile further on the walker or the boatman will come across a weir on the right, which marks the spot where a couple of right-angled bends in the old river forced the navigators to dig a short, straight cut across the loop. Then they had to build Ricketts Lock to effect the junction with the river again at the lower level. Here one can cross the canal by a bridge built at the end of the eighteenth century especially for canal traffic. From it the Langford waterworks to the north-east can be seen clearly.

The remarkable development of these waterworks was a major step forwards in the provision of an excellent supply of water for domestic and industrial consumption to Essex and beyond. In 1924 the Southend Waterworks Company obtained an Act of Parliament which allowed them to take water from the rivers Chelmer and Blackwater for treatment and subsequent distribution throughout its area. In 1928 the South Essex Waterworks Company followed their lead and obtained permission to take water from the river Stour at Langham. After the drought of 1934 further arrangements were made for more extraction and greater storage. Additional powers were sought and gained by the two companies for the Hanningfields scheme of 1950 and the Ely-Ouse scheme which used existing rivers and pipes to carry more water down to Langford for treatment.

The original works were abandoned in 1970 when a completely new system of water treatment was put in hand, and the modernization of this plant included a booster pumping station at Hullbridge, ten miles away, which is remotely controlled by radio from Langford. Langford Mill was bought by the water authority in 1924. All its original machinery was removed and a pump was installed to extract water. The millpond acts as a reservoir and the weir allows excess water to return to the main stream of the Blackwater.

Anglian Water produces a wide range of publications on the supply of water and on the rivers in their care, ranging from *A Reminder to Boat Owners* to *The Anglian Environment*, with emphasis on the care taken to preserve the wildlife and the character of the land and water. It also offers helpful literature like *Anglers' Choice*, which suggests alternatives to lead weight, compiled by the RSPB and the National Federation of Anglers.

An expert on the fishing to be had on both rivers and canal is Ted Pearson whose years of experience with the Essex Rivers Board and its successor Anglian Water, coupled with his obvious interest in the wildlife of the rivers, make his observations authoritative. The deep, slow moving water of the canal encourages bream and roach, and the fish which feed upon them, perch and pike. Carp and tench are also to be found, as well as the more common species such as gudgeon, minnow, stickleback and some crayfish. Most popular with the angler are roach and bream, though many people enjoy a tussle with the sharp-toothed pike, which are found evenly spread throughout the canal from Chelmsford to Heybridge.

The Blackwater, coming in at Langford, is still a river in its natural state, faster flowing, more shallow and, for the most part, with a gravel bed; this is an environment suitable for chub and dace. Roach have been caught here and in some deep sections the conditions allow bream to flourish, along with the predators pike and perch, but none of them in very large numbers.

The upper reaches of the Chelmer, above the canal, are populated by the same kinds of fish as the Blackwater, though chub are not so plentiful. One unusual fish to be discovered in the Chelmer is the brown trout, in very small numbers. They owe their presence to the Essex Rivers Board, who when they were responsible for these rivers introduced rainbow and brown trout to the Chelmer above Felsted as part of a breeding programme. The rainbow trout, not indigenous, could not breed in the conditions; the brown trout did, but only intermittently, so they are what might be called a wasting asset.

Anglian Water will restock any river with indigenous coarse fish but not with game fish such as trout. It encourages the public to report the moment a dead fish is seen because that can be the first indication of some pollution which must be attended to at once. Experience has shown that the public co-operates so willingly and promptly that Anglian Water can rely on their vigilance. When the pollution is traced and rectified the restocking begins.

Watch anglers intent upon the river and you will see a man making his way from one group to another. He is the bailiff, offering day tickets to those who are not members of the various clubs, and checking that they have an official rod licence issued by Anglian Water. Such firm control is essential in the proper administration of angling and is in the interest not only of the anglers and the general public but also of the fish and the flora and fauna of the river landscape. We were fascinated to hear from Ted that occasionally salmon, just a few, will run up the Blackwater to Beeleigh. In former days experts from the river authority would strip a female salmon of its eggs by simply smoothing its sides to effect the ejaculation, then fertilize them with the milt stripped from a male in a similar way. The eggs were then developed in a hatchery and the adult fish were eventually released. The salmon which may be seen these days are not the progeny of such parents; they are fish which have been thrown off course from their spawning grounds by floodtides, storms or other hazards. Ted Pearson reminded us that the water industry is in a state of flux at the moment. Privatization means that water supply and sewage treatment will be the concern of a public limited company, while rivers, flood prevention and sea defences will be the responsibility of the National Rivers Authority.

Opposite the mill at Langford is a drive with a public right of way running between the Blackwater on the west and the Langford Cut on the east that leads to the junction of the Blackwater with the canal. In a complicated triangle of watercourses the canal runs on through a lock with one of the original brick-arched bridges above it and heads on in a dead straight line to a point just west of Black Bridge in Heybridge, where, via an excavated channel, it reaches the tidal estuary of the Blackwater at Heybridge Basin.

At that same triangle, through a system of sluices, the Chelmer is released from its bondage as a canal, passes the former mill at Beeleigh Falls and runs into the tidal waters of the estuary. The Blackwater, which now produces the flow for the canal, joins it here at Beeleigh Falls, where its surplus water is shed over the weir. This stream flows on to the estuary so the two rivers make Beeleigh Falls House an island. The complicated flow of these waters, the Chelmer, the canal, the Blackwater, the Langford Cut and the tidal lagoon, once known as Beeleigh Harbour, has to be seen to be understood. It is a fascinating place for a walk when the rivers are swollen after rain. Then the water is an inspiring sight as it pours over Long Weir under the long footbridge. The original wooden bridge, built at the end of the eighteenth century, was swept away in the severe flood of 1947.

There are some wonderful walks hereabouts. One of them winds round from the old bridge over the canal, across Long Weir, up to the lock and then left to pass through a little copse overlooking the wide tidal basin, which spreads out below Long Weir. The bridge over the sluice offers a pleasing view across it. Here the Chelmer, freed at last from the canal, was sent through the last millrace on its course. The rush of the millstream from Beeleigh Mill caused such a backwash, such a scouring effect, that the bed of the "harbour" had to be

One of the original bridges over the canal at Beeleigh.

protected by a wide area of planking immediately below the sluice. That
planking is now but a broken framework, seen only at low tide. Also visible then
are the stone blocks set up in rows, reminiscent of the Giant's Causeway in
miniature, to take over the function of that timberwork.

The footpath runs on to another sluice where the millrace began. The
bridge here is private property, the entrance to Beeleigh Falls House. The mill
beside it boasts a colourful history. Its wheel was turning more than five hundred
years ago, for we know it was built and operated by the monks of Beeleigh Abbey
until their order was dispossessed around 1537. Hervey Benham puts it neatly:
"The monastery died but the mill developed into perhaps the greatest of all the
Essex country river mills, and certainly one of the most fascinating for the charm
of its situation, the richness of its record and the unique legacy it has
bequeathed."

The mill was built and rebuilt up to the beginning of the nineteenth century
when a definitive, grand new mill was erected, five storeys high. Shortly after
1845 a line steam-engine was installed in a separate engine house. Then, in 1875,
disaster struck. Somehow or other the huge timber-framed and weather-
boarded mill caught fire and was burned to the ground.

Pc Coult was on his beat in New London Road, a mile away in Maldon, when
he saw the glare of the fire. The alarm was raised and off went the Maldon Fire

Brigade, followed swiftly by the pump of the Essex and Suffolk Equitable Insurance Society. They fought a losing battle, for the fire, seen from as far away as Colchester, caused the collapse of the floors on which tons of grain and of finished sacks of flour were stored. The great weight of debris crashed down through the bridge, smashing into and setting on fire two lighters which were moored there. By the early morning light the devastation was seen to be so complete that nothing was left but a "large, smouldering heap."

The positioning of the Maldon pump had, however, been inspired. It pumped water continuously over the mill, with its five pairs of stones, and the separate steam-engine house. All the machinery was preserved intact though the roof was burned through and the windows were shattered by the heat. Furthermore the fire was prevented from spreading, via a tarred shed, to the house itself. The water-mill was not rebuilt and the steam-mill was demolished some twenty-five years ago, when the millstream was filled in. However, the engine-house is still there in the garden of the mill house now called Beeleigh Falls House. Sue Nelson and her friends were having lunch on the lawn in this idyllic spot on their own small island. They allowed us to poke about to see where the Chelmer joined the flow of water from Long Weir and became tidal, and to penetrate the undergrowth to photograph the Elephant boiler deep in its pit, where it supplied the steam for what the expert calls ". . . an 1845 Wentworth compound beam engine . . . geared to drive five stones mounted on a circular iron pedestal". Because both boiler and engine have been preserved intact this has been described as one of the county's "outstanding treasures of industrial archaeology".

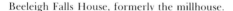

Beeleigh Falls House, formerly the millhouse.

The remains of the steam engine in the garden at Beeleigh Falls House.

The path winds on to broaden into a lane where Beeleigh Grange stands, hiding its old face behind the trees. It has a connection with the lions in Trafalgar Square. They were designed by Sir Edwin Landseer (1802–73), acknowledged to be the greatest animal painter of his time. In his early career he was a frequent guest for long periods at the Grange, home of his friend Mr W. N. Simpson. A grange was originally the farmhouse of an abbey, including all the outbuildings associated with a farm. The corn grown in the fields about the abbey and beside the rivers was harvested and brought in countless waggon-loads to the capacious barns where it was threshed through the winter months and sent in batches to Beeleigh Mill. It is hard to believe that the footpath we have trodden was, over a hundred years ago, a busy roadway, with heavy waggons and their horse teams ploughing up the muddy surface as they took grain to be ground, brought back flour, took coal to the new-fangled steam-mill and passed on through to business on the canal and in the fields. Now it is literally a backwater of history and a pleasure to stroll through with these thoughts in mind.

The remains of the Abbey itself can be seen by continuing down the lane, Abbey Turning, and taking the first road on the left, Beeleigh Chase, where the signpost points to Beeleigh Abbey. Through the graceful iron gates and just a stone's throw down the drive one can see the amazingly beautiful house, owned for many years by the Foyle family of London bookshop fame.

Beeleigh Abbey: this beautiful house has, on occasion, been open to the public.

What we would see today if we could tour the present house, which has on occasion been opened to the general public, is a spacious, comfortable home built around the remains of the Abbey—the chapter-house and the undercroft, or vaulted underpinnings of the dormitory, built around 1250. The big fireplace in the undercroft may indicate that this room also served as the calefactory, the warming room where the monks could come from their winter-cold cells to an all-too-brief period of welcome warmth. Carved on the stone surround is a group of figures, angels in appearance, playing the musical instruments of the day.

In the dorter, or dormitory, William Foyle housed his wonderful personal library. It was a great privilege to be a member of a group of librarians who were shown the house and the treasures of his library more than twenty years ago. To be allowed to handle a rare early edition of Chaucer was an unforgettable experience.

The house was extended in the sixteenth century by the new, lay owner who had a timber-framed wing built on. The stout old timbers with brick infilling complement the older Abbey remains with their stone doorways in rubble walls under steep-pitched roofs, making the picturesque whole a photographer's dream. Retracing our footsteps we follow the canal down the old towpath where it forms the boundary of Maldon golf-course.

The nine-hole course of the Maldon Golf Club is in a beautiful setting bounded by the Chelmer to the north and west and the canal to the east, with no roads anywhere near it. The club was formed as early as 1891; by the time it celebrates its centenary the great landmark here, the old railway viaduct, with its broken arch where it bestrides the river, will have been demolished to provide a bypass to relieve the appalling pressure of traffic on Maldon's town centre.

The old railway station on the Witham and Maldon branch of the Eastern Region of British Rail, south-east of the golf-course, was called Maldon East and Heybridge, but Heybridge itself is well beyond it, along the Causeway over Hey Bridge which crosses the Blackwater. Some might say it is a low-lying place without much character, but not those who know its age and history. From the bridge one can see the river, tidal here, on its last windings to the estuary, with a strong sea-wall running south-east from Hall Road for half a mile or more, leaving a great stretch of saltings and creeks, where the tide furrows the mud like the wrinkles on an old sailor's face.

The parish church is not spotted by the motorists who circle the roundabout beyond the bridge, yet it is very close by, tucked away behind trees and shrubs off Heybridge Street. It was built by the Normans late in the twelfth century on the site of the church built by the Saxons, who called their settlement here Tidwoldington after Tidweald their leader. It kept that name until well into the thirteenth century. Then the marvel of the new bridge arching over the Blackwater, all made of stone, with five arches, became the best-known landmark for travellers, so that in time the place itself became known as "Highbridge". This place had seen plenty of such travellers, for it was a port giving the British tribes access to trade with Gaul and the emerging Roman empire some four hundred years before the birth of Christ.

The second, Norman, church had a tower two and a half times the height of the present one. It was impressive but improvident, bearing in mind the village's situation on the edge of a vast marsh. One day, around 1450, wind, rain and tide combined to create a flood which was so severe that it caused the Blackwater to be diverted into the Chelmer's channel at Beeleigh. The rushing waters washed around the tower, undermined it and brought it crashing down upon the nave. By the end of the century, and through the generosity of Henry, Lord Bourchier, Earl of Essex, who died in 1483, the church was wholly rebuilt and back in use again. Much of the old material was salvaged and the nave was rebuilt to a reduced height.

In terms of population Heybridge never was a large village. Up to the coming of the canal it centred on the church and on the mill with Holloway Road and Heybridge Street meeting the Causeway between them. The mill has gone, torn down in 1954 after being idle for twelve years.

At the other end of the village, down Hall Road, the influence of the canal can be seen. On one side old cottages and the public house back on to the Blackwater. Opposite them an industrial estate has sprung up, facing on to the canal. Beyond it stands Heybridge Hall, midway between river and canal.

The canal by Bentall's former factory at Heybridge. The bridge built by Essex County Council can be seen in the distance.

The Heybridge Iron Works was started as a foundry at Goldhanger by William Bentall well before 1805. By that time he was able to see how much easier carriage of his raw materials and his finished products would be by the new canal. So he moved over to Heybridge to its very bank. The business prospered. The first large-scale Ordnance Survey map of 1874 showed the works to have spread round three sides of the parish churchyard, hemming it in against the main road. Bentall's frontage to the canal was in a wide arc from Black Bridge round to Goldhanger, or Wave Bridge and beyond, covering a total of more than thirteen acres. Here later generations of the Bentall family made all kinds of agricultural implements, including the Bentall broadshare plough of which fourteen thousand were sold in the eight years following its introduction in 1846.

In order to house the machines and implements they produced, prior to export via the canal all over the world, Bentall's had the huge warehouse built, in classical style and yellow brick, right by the canal and the road at Wave Bridge. That was in 1863. Since then its use has changed more than once, but its survival is ensured through its designation as an "ancient monument". The bridge itself, taking all the extra traffic generated by the industrialization of Heybridge, became unsafe. The County Council had it rebuilt and re-opened on 1st September, 1910.

From here the walker can take the straightest of lines down the towpath to the last lock on the canal at Heybridge Basin. The motorist has a circuitous route to follow along the Goldhanger road and down Basin Road. How thankful the engineers and the backers must have been when they saw the last lock-gates close on the waters of the estuary to allow the first boats and barges to be lifted on the ladder of locks which would finally take them to the wharves at Springfield, to disgorge vast quantities of grain, coal, chalk, lime, stone and manufactured goods of all kinds.

The Basin was a completely wild and undeveloped spot until the canal was built. There was nothing but the muddy foreshore of the river Blackwater into which the marshes drained. The opposition of the Borough of Maldon to the canal terminating anywhere near the town meant that the company had this long straight trench to dig through virgin soil, but at least there were no buildings to be circumvented, no rights to be negotiated and no roads to be bridged or diverted.

The houses and the two public houses here all postdate the construction of that last lock-gate in 1793. The pretty, weather-boarded cottages are the first houses on the site. The Old Ship Inn started out as the Brig Inn, opened in 1799. Ships as big as brigs could pass through the lock and lie in the basin whilst unloading to barges. The Brig failed, but eventually opened up again as the Old Ship in 1906 to serve a new public—people at leisure, boating, fishing or walking.

Looking towards the estuary from the last lock at Heybridge basin.

Now the hinterland has been developed and an estate of houses and roads cover the marshes. Owners of these desirable modern residences will know nothing of the days from 1823 to 1836 when Basin Road, then called Borough Marsh Road, was made a toll road without legal sanction. The toll-house still stands on the corner by the main road. The grip of the toll-collector was broken in 1836 by a crowd who, with two Justices of the Peace to see fair play, broke down the toll-gate and drove a cart down to the Basin and back to emphasize their right to do so at all times. With this right established more houses were built behind the Basin in the second half of the nineteenth century. Those canal builders did not imagine that such a road would be made, let alone that their canal would so soon be overtaken by the speed of rail transport. They could never have envisaged the forest of masts of pleasure boats from dinghies to cruisers anchored along the banks of the canal with not a company barge in sight!

CHAPTER SEVEN

The North Bank of the Blackwater Estuary

FROM Heybridge Basin we can follow the estuary, the combined flow of the two rivers, the canal and the surging tides of the North Sea, to Tollesbury and the open waters of the English Channel. On the further side of the B1026 as one turns out of Basin Road stands Saltcote Hall. This name is a reminder of the salt-works which were here and likewise at Maldon, but they have completely disappeared. They were the last connection with a form of salt manufacture so ancient that only limited archaeological evidence exists to hint at its importance.

The start of the story is intriguing. The first volume of the *Victoria History of Essex*, published in 1903, talks of "Red Hills", "the mysterious low mounds which abound on the borders of creeks and rivers of the Essex coast." Though described as hills, these mounds are no more than two to five feet high, but they spread very widely, from half an acre to some thirty acres. Local people took them for granted. At that time the editor could find no-one to help him in establishing their origin. The Reverend J. C. Atkinson, as early as 1880, had suggested that they might be some kind of saltworks, but the editor preferred the view that they were potters' sites.

The mounds occur on the coast from Burnham round to Walton-on-the-Naze, with an extra large number here on the north bank of the Blackwater estuary from Goldhanger to the Tollesbury marshes. Even as the editor wrote they were still being dug away to spread on the land because their ashy content was such a useful dressing for the stiff London Clay. By 1963 and the third volume of the *Victoria County History* more information had come to light. Thirteen Red Hills were plotted in Goldhanger alone. They were found to consist of burnt earth with many pieces of burnt clay and fragments of pottery of the Iron Age and later. In 1906 a special committee examined them in detail. Its members came to the conclusion that these were sites where seawater was boiled away in wide, shallow, pottery pans to leave a residue of that valuable commodity, salt.

Behind Saltcote Hall and on up to Slough House Farm great tracts of water mark the sites of gravel extraction, which still goes on. It was the preparation for further extraction which brought to light a Roman well some ten feet deep with its timber sides quite complete, preserved through the air-excluding density of the waterlogged earth. In a race against time, for gravel extraction is a commercial undertaking with financial implications, the county archaeologists discovered another well, predating the Roman occupation by a couple of thousand years; the shards of pottery recovered from it confirm a Bronze Age settlement with people continuing to live here until Saxon times, proved by the debris from iron-making found in a pit which was dug out around 500 AD.

Heybridge's Mill Beach recalls in its name a tidal mill long since gone and replaced by a caravan and holiday home complex. Holidaymakers can climb the sea-wall and look out over Colliers Reach, where the sailing coasters once queued up to discharge their coal into barges from the Basin. Further along the sea-wall, after a breezy, bracing walk, the view improves at Decoy Point. This headland owes its name to the horseshoe-shaped stretch of water which is the remains of a decoy pond. Until the beginning of this century ducks were lured into nets here in vast numbers and slaughtered for sale in the London markets. For the motorist to reach this spot he has to find his way past another big caravan park to come to the sea-wall, but it is worth the effort because this is where the causeway leaves the sea-wall and runs out to Osea Island.

Standing on the sea wall, looking across to Osea Island, one can easily suffer an optical illusion. The stony causeway seems to rise mysteriously from the waters rather than the tide ebb slowly away. Watching the snaking progress of the causeway as it lifts itself above the waves makes one realize the foolishness of attempting to cross until the causeway is high and dry, for one false move when the tide is lapping over it could bring disaster.

It is reckoned that the causeway is passable for four hours only at each tide. As far as the general public is concerned this fact is almost academic, for the island, owned now by Cambridge University, has been declared wholly private. Its farm manager and nine other people are Osea's sole population, working a farm covering some two hundred acres with another forty acres of pasture under the sea walls. Yet the island is not entirely private, for the university rents out four holiday cottages. The lucky tenants can see rare breeds of sheep and pigs, walk around their kingdom for a week or two and feel like regular castaways. The peace of the place is almost tangible.

Osea Island has had a chequered history. It was the Romans who first built the causeway and called the island Uvesia, though there is little evidence to be found of their occupation. William the Conqueror claimed it for himself and gave it to his nephew. It has been owned through the centuries by noble families including the Earl of Essex. Daniel Defoe (1660–1731) wrote of the vast flocks of wildfowl which took refuge there.

Very early in this century the island was bought by Mr F. N. Charrington of the brewing family. He saw and appreciated the problems and the heartache of alcoholism before he was twenty. He said later that he was converted to the temperance movement when he saw a woman begging for bread for her children outside the public house in which her husband was boozing. He came out and knocked her down. Charrington declared: "That blow knocked her into the gutter and me out of the brewery." He sold his interest in the firm for close on a million pounds and applied the money to campaigning for temperance. He bought Osea Island and set up on it a treatment centre for alcoholics, described then as "a home for gentlemen suffering from the baneful and insidious effects of alcohol". The trouble was that fishermen were always ready to smuggle in a bottle or two of the hard stuff. Even the old carter who took provisions across the causeway from the mainland could be "bought" at a very reasonable price.

So, whilst the well-intentioned Mr Charrington was doing his best to "dry out" men who were soaking in alcohol, the carter, who liked a drop himself, was undoing all his good work. One day, so the story goes, he was so drunk coming across the causeway, with the tide already up to the wheel hubs, that he fell overboard and the horse plodded on to make the mainland just in time. No-one seems to know what happened to the carter! Mr Charrington's experiment was doomed in any case, for the island was turned into an extensive naval base during the First World War when over two thousand sailors were stationed here. Today it is such a peaceful place, especially out of season, that the visitor leaves with reluctance.

At the south end of the village of Goldhanger are the three main meeting places.

Goldhanger lies for the most part off the main road. Its three historical meeting places for local gossip, the church, the inn and the village pump, stand near each other at the south end of the village, from whence there are wonderful walks out across the fields to the east and in both directions along the seawall under breezy, lonely skyscapes of unbelievable immensity. The old village pump with its big handwheel, like the old-fashioned diver's air-pump, stands facing the Chequers; as if to protect it from passing traffic there stands a semi-circle of granite, reputed to be half of a cidermill brought to the village by sea in the unremembered past. The church of St Peter is at the top end of Fish Street; the square was a very busy place when fishermen landed their catch and set up their market. Around a century ago one could see a thriving heronry and a decoy which yielded scores of ducks.

East of Goldhanger low-lying fields crouch behind the sea-wall beyond which the saltings spread, inundated at high tide, dangerous places with impassable creeks and bottomless mud-flats. Tollesbury can be reached by walking along the sea-wall, but the best way is via the B1026 to Tolleshunt D'Arcy and the B1023 from the middle of the village. Though it does not border the Blackwater estuary we can note as we pass through that more than one well-known person has lived in Tolleshunt D'Arcy.

First and foremost was the D'Arcy family, founded by the Norman knight who threw in his lot with William the Conqueror. Some two centuries later it was Robert D'Arcy, a lawyer's clerk married to the widow of John Ingal, a rich Maldon merchant, who made the family fortune and left one son squire of Danbury and the other John D'Arcy of Tolleshunt. The family spread around the county, but by the last years of the sixteenth century the Tolleshunt branch had withered. That past grandeur is recalled in D'Arcy Hall where a large part of the old house built around 1500 still stands firm. The drive crosses a bridge of banded brick and stone over the well-preserved moat. The sturdy bridge with four round arches, very satisfying to the eye, is dated 1585. In the grounds was grown the D'Arcy Spice apple which is still prized as a rare variety.

The man who lived in the village in modern times and won the hearts of folk for miles around was the dashing Doctor Salter. He came here as a new young doctor in October, 1864, and was received "with great cheering at the entrance to the village", as he says in his diary. He kept that diary going until the day before he died on 17th April, 1932. He was still Tolleshunt D'Arcy's doctor when he wrote on 23rd October, 1931: "Up early and had a long, old-fashioned round." He was then eighty-nine!

In his house came to live Margery Allingham (1904–66), the celebrated detective-story-writer. She also wrote a book about the village, set during the last war and called *The Oaken Heart*.

The road to Tollesbury is narrow with right-angled bends, showing very clearly its ancestry in days when the plodding horse and cart dictated the width and alignment of a road. The new generation of commuters must be frustrated by the limitations of this lane, Tollesbury's life-line through the low-lying fields. In former days this little town looked across the marshes and down the creeks for its livelihood from the Blackwater and the sea beyond. Its principal industry then was the dredging of oysters. This succulent bi-valve was an everyday dish in the meal of ancient British and Roman settlers in Essex. Up to the early years of this century it was a growth industry and the Pont, an area at the mouth of the Blackwater, was one of the most prolific oyster-growing grounds, where dredging was carried out on a free-for-all basis.

Private oyster-layings existed at Tollesbury where the oyster spat were grown to a suitable size, then harvested. An Act of 1868 gave a private company a monopoly on a 350-acre area of the bed of the Blackwater from Maldon right out to Tollesbury. Ten years later The Tollebsury and Blackwater Fishery established another area of oyster lanes. Their oysters were even exported to Russia as a great delicacy.

Take a walk round Tollesbury Marina and you will see hundreds of boats tied up here, with constant traffic between ship and shore. This safe harbour, at

The welcoming Tollesbury Marina.

the head of Woodrolfe Creek, has taken the place of the former shipyard. Seven acres of saltings were excavated to accommodate over two hundred and forty boats—perhaps we should call them yachts—drawing up to seven feet of water when lying afloat, with egress and ingress on the rising tide. Woodrolfe Boatyard, which runs the marina, is close at hand to supply and service all these sleek vessels.

We were heading that day landwards and westwards to the centre of town. First we passed the sail-lofts, all in timber and so tall. They were later used as marine stores, then fell into a dilapidated state. Now they are in excellent condition.

Passing the outskirts of Tollesbury, with many a new house indicating the increasing popularity of the place, we arrived at the shops in the wide, wide street which was once the village green, and at the parish church of St Mary which has been standing there for nearly a thousand years. The nave and the tower have survived all that time, though the latter was made taller, with brickwork, around 1600. A steady stream of people headed for the church porch and morning service.

Tollesbury Sail Lofts; now used as marine stores.

We were just in time, with the kind permission of the Reverend K. Lovell, to photograph the font. It is not an ancient or particularly fine font, but it is inscribed with a message which has an interesting story behind it. We read: "Good people all I pray take care, That in ye church you do not sware, As this man did." The story is told in the register of baptisms under 30th August, 1718:

> Elizabeth, daughter of Robert and Eliza Wood, being ye first childe whom was baptised in the New Font which was bought out of five pounds paid by John Norman, who some months before came into the church and cursed and talked loud in the time of Divine service, to prevent his being prosecuted for which he paid by agreement the above said five pounds. Note that the wise rhymes on the font were put there by the sole order of Robert Joyce then churchwarden.

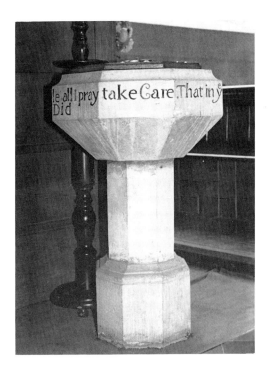

The font at St Mary's church, Tollesbury.

A little further down, on the other side of the street, is Station Road. It was a busy thoroughfare when folk came off the train on their way to and from work, the shops, and the connection to the wider world at Kelvedon. Tollesbury was the terminus of the light railway from Kelvedon, known by one and all as the Crab and Winkle line, run by the Great Eastern Railway and opened in 1904. It was extended from the village to the sea-wall in 1907 when a wooden pier was built, so it can be claimed to be the last privately-financed rail-sea link introduced into this country.

113

One of the men behind this venture was Arthur Wilkin, for the very good reason that he had established his fruit farm at Trewlands in Tiptree and built his jam-making factory in 1885, taking over Tiptree Hall farm as business developed. The extension was a failure, though the logistical requirements of the First World War helped keep the line open. In 1921 a halt was called and the pier was closed, though it was not actually demolished until thirty years later. The passenger service from Tollesbury to Kelvedon carried on until 1951, when it was declared too uneconomic to continue. The very last train on the line, taking a cargo of Wilkin's conserves from Tiptree to Kelvedon, stopped there for good in 1962.

Lines on the map still show part of the course of that railway. We found that the best way to appreciate its effect on the landscape was to walk the footpath which runs at the side of Mell Farm, at the southernmost point of Tollesbury. Mell is an early spelling of mill, and with Mill Creek and Mill Point south of the farm, on the Blackwater, there is no doubt that a very ancient tide mill once worked here. The footpath runs about half a mile to the east and there you see the shallow cutting dug out for the railway, running north-west past a great gun tower of the last war and south-east through a field of sheep to the bank of the Blackwater.

All is perfect peace here. Tollesbury Wick Marshes blend into a great skyscape which shrinks the grey bulk of Bradwell Power Station into a misty smudge on a horizon of sea and sky in ever-changing subtleties of light and shade and colour. An inspiring place to say a lingering farewell to the north bank of the ever-widening Blackwater estuary.

CHAPTER EIGHT

The South Bank of the Blackwater Estuary

I T IS difficult to understand why the Blackwater gave its name to the estuary, rather than the Chelmer, for a glance at the map shows the Chelmer flowing straight and clear of the bonds of the canal, past Beeleigh Abbey, under Fullbridge at the foot of Market Hill to the point where the writhing Blackwater joins it opposite the recreation ground overlooked by Downs Road. However, the river is then called the Blackwater and we shall follow it as it passes Hythe Quay and washes the shores of Northey Island.

Maldon is an ancient borough. Its history is too long to relate here and its surviving buildings are so varied in age and architectural importance that we cannot do justice to them in the course of our riverside peregrinations. An excellent guide to the town and its associated villages has been prepared by the Maldon District Council, along with trails and footpath leaflets, so let us look at the town simply in its relationship to the river.

At the Fullbridge we can see at low tide the mud which caused the Saxons to christen this difficult crossing "the bridge over the mud". Anyone who has seen the flooding river meeting the racing tide will appreciate that this bridge has needed rebuilding any number of times. Even the road itself had to be raised as a causeway to keep the connection between Maldon and Heybridge. Fullbridge was a wooden construction in 1800 when it was rebuilt, but by 1822 it was almost worn out again. This time they tried wood and iron. Unfortunately the old and the new materials did not marry well together, and within fifty years, in 1876, tenders had to be invited for another rebuilding. This time the technique of working in iron, after years of experience, was more perfectly understood; that bridge lasted until 1961, when ever-increasing traffic made further rebuilding necessary.

By the bridge a footpath climbs the bank, giving a clear view over the wharves and warehouses and the boat-connected businesses before meeting up with Downs Road. On the way the walker overlooks the premises of the Maldon Salt Company. Though no longer making red hills as the people of earlier times did, the company carries on the ancient industry by extracting sea-water at its saltiest from the estuary and evaporating it away in huge coppers, where ice-like crystals of salt form on the surface of the water in a kind of microcosm of the Arctic Circle. The end result is those characteristic boxes of sea-salt on sale in all the best stores.

115

From Downs Road it is but a step to Hythe Quay Road and the Hythe itself. That name is the Old English for a landing place, and the barges tied up here show the long tradition of trade from this wharf. This was where the barges unloaded their cargoes of coal and chalk for the fires and the limekilns of the town. A map made in 1516 shows "The Towne's Coleheape and Chalkheape" on this spot, and several wharves let out by the borough to the traders of the time.

Adjacent to the Hythe and very convenient for the clinching of business deals on the wharf was, and still is, the Queen's Head. The earliest document in the deeds of this inn is dated 25th May, 1700. It shows the relationship of the inn to the wharves when it was sold as a "messuage and Wharfs or Keys called Harrington Key, Darcyes Key alias Darceys Wharf and Bourchiers Key with a Lime Kiln near adjoining it."

It is believed that in the eighteenth century the Queen's Head acted as a kind of "decontamination centre" for seamen arriving from foreign parts. They would be examined here for freedom from disease before being let loose on unsuspecting Londoners. It is thought that this inn had a "tidal licence" allowing seafarers to go ashore to eat and drink then be away again on the next tide. There were times then when the tide flowed right into the inn!

From the Hythe the quay runs on to turn into a promenade which was opened on 26th June, 1895, when Maldon Borough Council laid out fourteen acres of land to provide a recreation ground with a bathing pool and rowing

The causeway to Northey Island.

boats for hire. At the celebratory luncheon the MP Cyril Dodd declared that "if young Londoners knew what boating, fishing and bracing air were to be enjoyed at Maldon, Maldon would soon become a London suburb." Further on one can walk out to a spit of land beyond the sea-wall where all thoughts of people and their noisy activities can be lost to sight and sound as one looks east towards Northey Island and the wide tidal waters of the estuary.

A bracing walk along the sea-wall of a mile or so brings the visitor to the causeway which connects the island with the southern bank of the Blackwater. Motorists have to make their way out of Maldon via the B1018 towards Latchingdon. It is easy to miss the drive to South House Farm—and thus to Northey Island—because it is hidden by a long row of houses on either side. At the farm itself, cars must be left at the roadside. Walkers can pass through the gate at the head of the drive because a public right of way exists over the farm road.

You are walking into history here, for this was the site, on the mainland somewhere beyond the farm (authorities do not agree on the exact site), where the Battle of Maldon was fought in 991. A permit is required before you can cross that inviting causeway. Applications should be addressed to the Warden, Northey Cottage, Northey Island, Maldon.

Our road runs on over Mundon Wash to Mundon itself, leaving a great triangle of land south of the Blackwater with but one narrow lane petering out at Brick House Farm, west of Lawling Creek. On the way there is White House Farm, home of the enterprising farmer John Marriage who in 1820 had his own canal built, based on the course of the Mundon Wash, to take his produce out and bring his coal and manure in from the Blackwater and its access to Chelmsford via the canal and London via the sea and the Thames. Though it was disused and derelict by the end of the century it was re-established by Anglian Water in the nineteen-seventies as part of a big drainage scheme.

Mundon itself lines the main road now, but time was when it centred only around the church and the school to the east. The way to reach them is off that same lane and the turning Old Church Road which bends round past one or two houses and the old rectory until it ends at Mundon Hall, a beautiful, secluded place and very different from its appearance some twenty years ago. Then the church right beside the Hall and the churchyard were completely overgrown; it was a blackberry-picker's paradise, even though four bulls were tethered alongside the footpath to discourage walkers. Now the Hall looks clean and bright and the neglected church of St Mary has been taken in hand by a band of hardworking volunteers. The footpath has been signposted so that one may walk along St Peter's Way which uses path, track and lane to arrive some miles later at St Peter's Chapel on the North Sea.

St Mary's was certainly worth preserving. Through the industry of these unsung volunteers the church will continue to display the expertise of its builders. It was built in the fourteenth century with a nave of rubble, covered with plaster, a roof of hand-made clay tiles and oak framing from the wood nearby. Other features, like the introduction of brick for the chancel in the eighteenth century, show the continuing care for the place as a religious community centre. Only in the present century, as the rural population declined and Mundon people found work and the focus of their daily lives in nearby towns, was the church allowed to become redundant and moulder away. Now local pride in such a possession has been rekindled and judging by the enthusiasm of the volunteers it would seem that the restoration of the church and its future maintenance is assured. The full architectural details are set out in the Department of the Environment's "List of Buildings of Special Architectural or Historic Interest".

Mundon Hall stands within the remains of its ancient moat, evidence of its Saxon origin when the moat marked territory, provided water, deterred attack or burglary and produced food in the form of fish and fowl. The Hall is not listed in the learned tomes on architecture, largely because it has always been a family home, built, rebuilt, altered and extended through the thousand years since the moat was excavated, to suit the needs of each generation.

At Latchingdon, beside the church, a road leaves the B1010 to run

St. Mary's church, Mundon, in the course of restoration.

Mundon Hall and its ancient moat in the foreground.

eastwards, keeping the Blackwater company at a safe and respectful distance all the way to Bradwell. Latchingdon is the only parish which can claim the Blackwater and the Crouch as its borders. It forms the narrow part, the neck as it were, of the Dengie Peninsula. The church, Christ Church, is an attractive landmark but of no great age, having been built in 1857 to replace the old church of St Michael, a mile away down Lower Burnham Road. This has been sold and converted into a house, and boasts inscriptions on its walls like: "Mathew Bets and Robert Pierc mad this wall 1618". The village itself, straggling down and around the corner of the main road, is developing rapidly. New houses of unusual design for rural location have sprung up like creations from those old-fashioned sets of Lott's bricks, beloved by children of an earlier generation.

The essential rural Essex soon appears again. The fields slope up on the left, hiding a view of the Blackwater, but up by Lawling Hall the river spreads out in a glorious panorama of liquid light and shining water under an ever changing sky. Lawling was a manor held in the fourteenth century by the Abbey of Christchurch, Canterbury. In 1332 the tenants of this manor were exempted from the ancient custom of having to provide a palfrey, or riding horse, for a new abbot on his appointment. The abbot's steward, Edward Gauge, interceded on behalf of the people of Lawling, not only because it was a poor place but also, possibly, because its animals had been struck down repeatedly by murrain, a deadly cattle disease.

A chapel stood here in the sixteenth century and at that time the area was described as Latchingdon and Lawling. Today the amalgamation of parishes is of Latchingdon and Snoreham. Court rolls still exist from the seventeenth century for the Manor of Lawling Hall, but the only tangible evidence of the old manor is the rather stark brickwork of the farmhouse still called Lawling Hall. We know that it was owned by the Earl of Warwick in 1669 because he was indicted by the manor court for "not repairing a cartbridge in Latchingdon cum Lawlyn in the grounds belonging to Lawling Hall, in the highway from Steeple to Maldon being much in decay and out of repair and very dangerous and almost unpassable".

From things past we drive very much into things present at Maylandsea where houses and holiday homes gather under the sea-wall which hems in Mundon Creek. The only way from there to Steeple is back along the road through Mayland to circumvent Mayland Creek. Mayland itself has a history of market gardens and nurseries where one can still buy good garden plants.

Steeple's parish boundary is the Blackwater, but the village keeps to the street and leaves the holiday homes, the caravans and the sailing and boating clubs to occupy the water's edge. The fact that the first settlers here built their homes on the highest land in the vicinity may account for the village's name. It is true that the church of St Lawrence and All Saints has a steeple, but it is a relatively new construction. The whole church is a rebuilding on a new site in 1884, using as much material as possible from the demolition of the old church. The result is a pretty little Christmas card church designed by Frederic Chancellor, an industrious Essex architect and, in 1888, first mayor of the newly incorporated Borough of Chelmsford.

There is a real variety of architecture to be enjoyed; perhaps the new and the old in Steeple are best represented in the Sun and Anchor public house and the two cottages labelled Sun and Anchor Cottage respectively which stand next to it. The public house was built in 1940, probably the only public house in the country to have been built during the war. The two cottages were once combined as the former inn. We know that it was in business at least as early as 1764 because it was then that Robert Church, Surveyor of Weights and Measures, reported that George Rowland of "ye Anchor" had "good" measures, which certainly was not always the case in those days.

To be at the centre of all the seaboard activity a visitor has to make his way down the road to Hill Farm and on up the narrowest of lanes to the holiday home and caravan park, where a bumpy ride over the "sleeping policemen" brings him to the sea-wall and beyond it to a primitive, small carpark where the estuarine Blackwater washes Lawling and Mayland Creeks. The peacefulness of

The friendly sailing club at Steeple Bay.

the place on a Sunday morning out of season draws many people here for a really quiet weekend. The clubhouse of the Steeple Bay Sailing Club has a friendly, comfortable air with all kinds of boats and nautical knick-knacks crowding its boat park, and a wonderful view from its second storey clubroom across the wide waters. The place has the charm of bygone days, with opportunities for the simple pleasures of walking, rowing, sailing, bird-watching or just sitting soaking up the sun and the scenery.

To follow the Blackwater we must go back again and on through Steeple to find another road, just past Gate Farm, which leads to the sea-wall by Stansgate Abbey Farm. A large notice dissuades "public vehicles" from passing beyond Steeple Wick because, apart from the farm, the only building here is the Marconi Sailing Club. Even the sea-wall footpath peters out by the farm, but stand at the end of that footpath and you can enjoy an inspiring view of the Blackwater flooding round Osea Island. There is a long vista down the estuary, busy with sailing craft from barges to sailboards, towards Tollesbury on the far shore and Bradwell on the far right. Perhaps the atmosphere here is refreshingly bright and cheerful because everybody comes here for one purpose—to enjoy themselves.

The tranquil view from Stansgate Abbey Farm across to Osea Island.

Just a little further east along the road to Bradwell another lane leads up to the banks of the Blackwater again, where an estate has grown up on Ramsey Island. The double yellow lines on the road right down to the public house at the Stone prove the popularity of this spot when the sun shines. Even in October powerboat enthusiasts are out in strength, zooming up and down in their sleek craft, some of them towing wet-suited water-skiers.

It is hard to believe that forty years ago this area was nothing but a wilderness of marsh and salting, for, according to the Maldon District Council guide, it is the "most populous part of the parish". The parish is St Lawrence, with its church to the south on top of a hill so surprisingly steep in this landscape that it caused the writer of a guide-book a hundred years ago to warn that: "A hill in this parish is steep, rutty and dangerous for bicyclists."

We come, via Bradwell Wick and Bradwell Hall, to the last village in the realm of the Blackwater. The Wick is well outside the village because it was, in the days of Saxon farming, the dairy-place, and since the cows and the sheep were milked out in the fields the "wick" developed from a shed to a hovel for the herdsmen and eventually to a large house in its own right. Unusually in Essex, the Hall is well away from the church of St Thomas, which has a tower built in

St Thomas the Apostle at Bradwell.

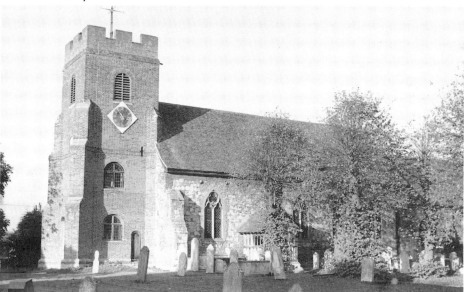

1706 and a nave and chancel showing again architect Chancellor's hand in the 1864 restoration of their fourteenth-century fabric. Three features illustrating aspects of past village life are to be seen against the churchyard wall. One is the large stone mounting-block by the south gateway; it was used by farmers and their ladies who had ridden from outlying hamlets of the parish to mount their horses and set out for home again after the service. The second is the remains of the stocks now built into the wall, and the third is the "cage", the tiny lock-up in which village rowdies and petty criminals cooled their heels until the constable could take them to Maldon or Chelmsford for questioning examination and further incarceration to await trial. It stands at the corner of the churchyard, a small brick building put up more than four hundred years ago and carefully restored in modern times. The tiles of its little roof harmonize with those of the row of equally old cottages standing beside it. The doorposts are the remains of the pillory, used to entrap the arms and present the back of those unfortunate people sentenced to be whipped. A pleasant walkabout will reveal other places in Bradwell worth seeing, including Bradwell Lodge with its prominent belvedere, a room built on the roof to provide a most wonderful viewing point. It was used

The village "cage" at Bradwell, where petty criminals were left to cool down.

The graveyard and a few of the houses surrounding it at Bradwell.

by Thomas Gainsborough (1727–88), the famous painter, as a studio when he stayed here for a while. It rather cunningly conceals the chimneys, one at each corner, seen as pillars. The Tudor origin of the house is hidden on the south side by additions built over five years from 1781 in Georgian style with classical motifs, to the designs of John Johnson, the architect of Chelmsford's Shire Hall.

His client was the newly-arrived Reverend Henry Bate-Dudley (1745–1824), later knighted, and one-time editor of the *Morning Post*. He was a great character who, in his spare time, enjoyed fox-hunting and writing plays or entertaining his friends here like Gainsborough, Garrick, Mrs Siddons and Hogarth. A competent farmer, he was in the vanguard of agricultural improvers, showing what could be done on a larger scale by reclaiming two hundred and fifty acres of marshland on his estate and introducing mole-draining.

From Bradwell Lodge, through the picturesque village street watched over by the church, the road runs on through history, as it were, to Bradwell Waterside. Once again, the problem for motorists is that they can drive right down the street, up over the sea-wall to the very water itself, but if they wish to park it is necessary to back up, turn round and retreat as far away, perhaps, as

125

the marina down by the coastguard station. The reasons for lingering at this end of Bradwell are many: the view across the estuary, the bird life to be observed, the walk along the sea-wall which can take you clear out to the North Sea and St Peter's Chapel, the opportunities for sailing and cruising, and the pleasure of food and drink at the old Green Man. Look across over Pewet Island directly north-west and your eye will be crossing the imaginary line which marks the boundary of the County of Essex on the river Blackwater.

Let us delay our goodbyes to the river, for just a little further on are two monuments to the past and the present which should be seen whilst we are in this remote corner of the county. The first, to the past, is a recently erected memorial, the representation of a plane, nose-dived to earth, on a paved plinth where a plaque is inscribed:

R. A. F.
BRADWELL BAY
1942–1945
THIS MEMORIAL HAS BEEN
ERECTED IN MEMORY OF
THE 121 MEMBERS OF THE
ALLIED AIR FORCES WHO IN
ANSWER TO THE CALL OF DUTY
LEFT THIS AIRFIELD TO FLY
INTO THE BLUE FOREVER

No-one who reads this plaque could leave this sad and lonely wayside memorial without conflicting emotions.

Not far from the memorial is one of the control towers of the airfield with an original airmen's hut beside it. Though the tower has been converted to a house, the wide sweep of long grass and the concrete roads still convey a little of that wartime atmosphere. Now the only people using it are learner-drivers getting ready for the real road and children from the nearby estate on their bicycles.

The road leads on to Bradwell Nuclear Power Station, surely a monument to man's mastery of the most complex scientific procedures in the production of electricity. Its mighty bulk and the low hum of its machinery make it seem like a friendly, sleeping giant. No-one can deny that it has brought employment to the area and an improvement in local services. The building, to the design of Maurice Bibb, was begun in 1957. Commissioned in 1962, the plant has operated well for twenty-two years and was working to full capacity at the time of writing. The Central Electricity Generating Board has issued a leaflet devoted to Bradwell Power Station which, it says, occupies about one-eighth of a square mile, with only a quarter of that space needing to be included in the special security area. The maximum output of the two reactors is 250 megawatts. When one considers that one kilogram of enriched uranium fuel produces as much electricity as 78 tonnes (76¾ tons) of coal, this must be a big factor in the reduction of chemical pollution of our atmosphere.

The capacious power station at Bradwell viewed from the sea wall.

Opposite: The war memorial erected at Bradwell Bay.

127

The leaflet gives further details of the construction of the various elements of the plant with an eye to maximum safety. When we read that a crane capable of lifting two hundred tons at a time was used to assemble the biological shield of the reactor building and to install the ninety-two foot high boilers, the magnitude of the undertaking and the sheer ingenuity of scientists and designers, engineers and architects begins to come home to us. The only way in which the Blackwater is affected is that waste heat, in the form of warm water, is discharged into it. After sixteen years of monitoring no effect at all on the marine environment has been detected. The public can visit the power station by arrangement over the telephone; as the Board says: "The best way to understand what goes on inside Bradwell is to come inside."

Throughout this book we have been walking in the footsteps of Arthur Shearley Cripps, a missionary in Africa whose memorial can be seen in the church at Ford End. From 1900 to 1927 and again from 1930 until the time of his death he served as a missionary in what was then Southern Rhodesia. He died out in Africa, blind and poor but with the love and respect of the people he had tried so hard to serve.

When he returned to Africa after a brief rest in Essex in 1906 he wrote a poem aboard the ss *Goorkha* which reflects our feelings after journeying down these two rivers. Four lines will suffice to sum up those feelings:

> England has greater counties,
> Their peace to hers is small,
> Low hills, rich fields, calm rivers!
> In Essex, seek them all. . .

Right: The canal upstream from Boreham Bridge

Select Bibliography

Addison, Sir William. *Essex Worthies*. 1973.

Benham, Hervey. *Some Essex Water Mills*. 2nd edn. 1983.

Booker, J. *Essex and the Industrial Revolution*. 1974.

Braintree and Witham Times. From 1929.

Braintree District Council. *Guide to the District*. Current edition.

Buckley, D. G., Editor. *Archaeology in Essex to AD 1500*. 1980.

Came, Peter. A History of the Chelmer and Blackwater Navigation Canal. (c. 1976).

Came, Peter. *Maldon and Heybridge in Old Picture Postcards*. 1985.

Chapman, John, and André, Peter. A map of the County of Essex from an actual survey taken in 1772–73 and 1774.

Christy, Miller. *Durrant's Handbook for Essex*. 1887.

Coller, D. W. *The People's History of Essex*. 1861.

Corke, David. *The Nature of Essex*. 1984.

Curtis, Gerald. *The Story of the Sampfords . . .* 1974.

Day, James Wentworth. *A Garland of Hops*. 1978.

Defoe, Daniel. *A Tour Through the Eastern Counties of England*. 1772.

Essex Chronicle. From 1764.

Essex Countryside. From 1952.

Essex County Council. *Essex Archaeology*. From 1984.

Essex Herald. From 1800 to 1943.

Essex Naturalist. From 1887 to 1956.

Essex Review. From 1892 to 1957.

Farries, K. G. *Essex Windmills, Millers and Millwrights*. 1988.

Jarvis, Stan. *Chelmsford in Old Picture Postcards*. 2nd edn. 1988.

Jarvis, Stan. *Dunmow in Old Picture Postcards*. 1986.

Jarvis, Stan. *A View into Essex*. 1979.

Jarvis, Stan. *W. & H. Marriage & Sons Ltd, 1824–1974*. 1974.

Kelly's Directories Ltd. Directories of Essex from 1845 to 1937.

Lucy, Isabel, and Gould, B. M. An Anthology of Essex. 1911.

Maldon and Burnham Standard. From 1959.

Maldon District Council. *Guide to the District*. Current edition.

Maunder, Samuel. *The Biographical Treasury*. 1866.

Maxwell, Donald. *Unknown Essex*. 1925.

Mee, Arthur, Editor. *The King's England*. 1951.

Morant, Philip. *The History and Antiquities of the County of Essex*. 1768.

Ordnance Survey. Maps 1 : 50,000, sheets 167 and 168.

Pevsner, Nikolaus. *The Buildings of England, Essex*. 2nd edn. 1965.

Reaney, P. H. *The Place-Names of Essex*. 1969.

Royal Commission on Historical Monuments. *An Inventory of the Historical Monuments in Essex*. 1923.

Smith, Donald. *Pigeon Cotes and Dove Houses of Essex*. 1931.

Taverner, James. *An Essay Upon the Witham Spa*. 1737.

Tompkins, Herbert W. *Companion into Essex*. 2nd edn. 1947.

Uttlesford District Council. *Guide to the District*. Current edition.

The Victoria History of the Counties of England. A History of Essex. From 1903.
Warwick, Frances, Countess of. *Life's Ebb and Flow.* 1929.
Wright, Thomas. *The History and Topography of the County of Essex.* 1831 and 1835.
Young, Arthur. *General View of the Agriculture of Essex.* 1807.

The *Victoria* on Paper Mill Lock.

Index

Illustrations in **bold type**

132

INDEX